4-17-07

Jon,

Thank you for y n
the Drive Test.

I hope you enjoy the book.

Best regards,

Hiring driven salespeople is critical to any company's growth and success. Croner and Abraham have hit upon powerful and practical techniques.

—Al Turnauer, Vice President, Sales, Vocollect

When companies apply science to managing salespeople, results come from a dependable process, not by chance.

—Cheryl Jekiel, Vice President and General Manager, Ralcorp

This book provides an insightful examination of a critical skill required by all successful businesses.

—James J. Fitzsimmons, President and CEO, GKN Aerospace—Aerostructures

When it comes to hiring salespeople, the cost of failure is simply unforgivable. There's no one better to provide direction on reducing that risk than Dr. Croner. Buy this book. Read it. Use it.

—Tammy Bitterman, Founder and Managing Partner, The Acceleration Group

Improving sales force productivity is one of the most powerful drivers of organic growth and share gain. This book provides managers with valuable tools to impact this issue early —at the time of hiring.

—Ross Rosenberg, Vice President, Business Development & Marketing, Danaher Corporation

Hiring the right salesperson is one of the most important and difficult decisions managers make. Hiring a candidate who lacks Drive can have a dramatic negative impact on any sales team. With so much at stake, sales managers would be wise to follow this practical guide to getting it right.

> —Kelly Grindle, Vice President, Motors Group,
>   Johnson Outdoors

Salespeople have tremendous impact on the fortunes of an enterprise. Croner and Abraham have provided an eminently practical guide that will prove invaluable to anyone looking to build a top-performing sales staff.

> —Thomas Gruenwald, Vice President,
>   Strategic Resources for Tellabs

Hiring underperforming salespeople creates financial hardship on large companies and small startups alike. This book provides a proven method for selecting talented candidates.

> —Neil Witmer, Ph.D., Principal, Witmer & Associates

NEVER

HIRE A BAD

SALESPERSON AGAIN

SELECTING CANDIDATES
WHO ARE ABSOLUTELY
DRIVEN TO SUCCEED

NEVER
HIRE A BAD
SALESPERSON AGAIN

SELECTING CANDIDATES
WHO ARE ABSOLUTELY
DRIVEN TO SUCCEED

DR. CHRISTOPHER CRONER
RICHARD ABRAHAM

Contents

Acknowledgments

I owe a debt of gratitude to numerous people. Thanks are owed first to Richard Abraham. Rick's vision and guidance inspired me to make my work and research on the Drive model of sales performance accessible in book form. I also thank Neil Witmer and Jeff Grip at Witmer & Associates. Neil and Jeff brought me on board to take over the sales assessment practice of the firm. Through that work, I originated the Drive model and received numerous invaluable experiences in psychological assessment. Neil's guidance and mentorship have been invaluable. I owe gratitude as well to the companies whose sales forces we have helped to upgrade—this book is dedicated to them. I also thank my parents, Don and Sally Croner, whose hard work, sacrifice, and dedication have formed the bedrock of my achievements and aspirations. Thanks to my brother Patrick, whose ambition, competitiveness, and optimism have provided strong moral support through the years. Also, thank you to my fellow students at Second City Training Center in Chicago. You have helped me take my performance to another level.

—Christopher Croner

I would like to thank every CEO, entrepreneur, and sales manager I have ever met who shared their triumphs, heartaches, and frustrations in trying to build a world-class sales team. This book is a tool for them, so that they can continue to take risks, invest with confidence, and realize their hard-fought hopes and dreams. Thanks are also owed to my collaborator, Dr. Chris Croner, whose high standards of research and quality have raised the bar for everyone interested in what makes salespeople run. Finally I would also like to thank my wife, Erin, and my children, Marlena and Katherine, who share and support my passion for knowledge and new ideas.

—Richard Abraham

Introduction

You're never there.

—Tiger Woods

Tiger Woods was in an especially good mood. He had recently completed what many golf historians agree was the finest run in his sport's history. Four major titles in a row! Seventeen PGA victories! Record-breaking tournament earnings!

Yet when a reporter from the *Chicago Sun-Times* asked him what was left for him to accomplish, Tiger flashed him an incredulous, "Are you serious?" look that came from deep within the burning soul of a man born to compete—and dominate.

"You're *never* there," reprimanded Tiger. "You can always be better the next day. That's how I look at golf and how I look at life. You can always, always be better. . . . If you think you can't, then walk, because you have no business being out here if you think you can't get any better. That's how I approach each and every practice session, each and every round I play."

Tiger Woods . . . Michael Jordan . . . Jackie Joyner-Kersee . . . Lance Armstrong . . . each born with God-given gifts of coordination, strength, endurance, and intelligence. Yet such supernatural physical abilities alone are not enough to push these magnificent athletes to the astonishing levels of performance they have achieved in their careers.

No, each superstar shares another ingredient, a white-hot fuel that turbocharges their natural gifts: the electrifying personality characteristic that psychologists call Drive. Drive is the common denominator found in nearly all high-performing achievers in any competitive field. In fact, Drive is so important, and so powerful, that it often pushes less-talented individuals beyond competitors who may have been born with higher skills but lack the burning desire to succeed.

And, as we will demonstrate throughout this book, it is Drive that is the most important characteristic in identifying and selecting people who can successfully sell for a living.

Why is Drive so important to successful selling? Because of all professions, sales requires the most intense self-motivation in the face of rejection, and because sales exerts the most grueling and constant pressure on self-esteem. Only people who love to compete, have supreme confidence in themselves, and are willing to laugh in the face of rejection have the constitution to survive and thrive in this most competitive of business environments.

It has been estimated that up to 50 percent of the people who are currently trying to make their living by selling are in the wrong line of work. They may be excellent communicators, gregarious, and likable, but they do not have, nor will they ever have, the Drive to provide a meaningful return on the huge investment you make in them. Sadly,

> **This book has been written for business owners, entrepreneurs, and managers who have suffered the frustration and financial heartbreak of placing the success of their life's work in the hands of salespeople who do not have the innate personality characteristics—aka Drive—to deliver.**

in a recent study, marketing professor Gilbert Churchill Jr. and his colleagues estimated that the expenses accrued in the recruiting, training, lost sales, and managerial time devoted to a bad hire often exceed $100,000 per salesperson.

Now, we would like you to slow down for a moment and read this very, very carefully: *It doesn't have to be that way in your company.* Through proper testing and interviewing techniques, salespeople with Drive *can* absolutely be identified, selected, and motivated to produce consistently, at high levels, for you and for your organization. While it takes time, patience, and discipline, it is possible to stock your team with A and B players—thoroughbreds—who have the intestinal fortitude and the burning will to succeed as high-producing salespeople.

A quick note of caution before we proceed: This book is not for the faint of heart. It is not for the business owner or manager who does not appreciate the supreme importance of the sales function. It is not for the sales manager who is in denial about the cost of hiring and carrying mediocre performers. It is not for the sales manager who may not have the heart to make tough decisions. These decisions can hurt when it comes to releasing people whom the manager may personally like but who should be pursuing a different line of work, for the benefit of every-one, including the employee.

Identifying, selecting, and retaining Driven salespeople is a rigorous process requiring patience, discipline, and focus. But the payoffs are *huge,* in terms of both higher revenues and lower costs, a combination rarely achievable in other areas of your business.

We therefore invite you to take this journey with us, a journey into the hearts and minds of people who sell for a living. We will show you why some win, some plateau, and some lose. Most importantly, we will show you how you can "stack the deck" with sales athletes who are born to run—for you!

Part One:

Elements of Drive

2

1
Chapter

Drive: The Foundation of Success

*There is no secret to my training regi-
men. I just make my practices tougher
than the races.*

—Lance Armstrong

What a brilliantly revealing statement from a man whose
actual races involved riding his bicycle up steep moun-
tains in France. But it's true! Lance Armstrong and other
high achievers drive themselves *beyond* their limits, not
just when the money is on the line but behind the scenes,
every day. They show their Drive in the relentless course
of their preparation, dedication, and training.

> **Drive—the Lance Armstrong type of Drive— is the most important factor for sales success. In a 1998 analysis of more than 45,000 salespeople, psychology professor Andrew Vinchur and his colleagues found need for achievement, a critical component of Drive, to be more predictive of sales success than any other trait.**

Drive is also essential in unleashing other sales skill sets. To be sure, relationship skills and persuasiveness are important. But these traits are simply not sufficient without Drive. Furthermore, you can provide salespeople with excellent training, but without Drive, the money is largely wasted. While it may seem counterintuitive, you will be better off in the long run if you hire a Driven person who has no sales experience and teach that person your business than if you hire a candidate who has experience but lacks Drive.

While successful salespeople have different styles, they almost always share the Drive personality trait. For example, as reported in 1994 by Geoffrey Brewer, the Gallup Management Consulting Group through two decades of research identified several skills critical to sales success. Two of those skills, intense motivation and disciplined work habits, are hallmarks of Drive.

Anatomy of a (Sales) Winner

Have you ever had the exquisite pleasure of managing one of the *great* salespeople? You know the type. They come in early and leave late. They drop in on weekends to handle "paperwork." During the week, they're always out with customers, on whose behalf they fight tenaciously. On the occasions when they do get rejected, they move on immediately (for surely the next sales call will be successful). And when they smell the goal line—the close—nothing and nobody can hold them back!

In the course of examining our own psychology practice, and considering more than 80 years of research in the sales sector, we now know that there is a consistent formula common to the personality of nearly all successful salespeople. They have three essential traits:

1. They are motivated by a need to achieve outstanding results, and they are willing to do virtually whatever it takes to succeed.

2. They love to compete, both with themselves and with others.

3. They are optimistic, that is, they are certain of their ability to *win*.

> **These three traits—need for achievement; competitiveness; and optimism—are *all* necessary elements of Drive.**

Need for Achievement

Top-gun salespeople have a burning *need* to achieve. They are ambitious, disciplined, and focused on advancement. You may laugh, at first glance, at the *disciplined* element, since on the surface, great salespeople may seem anything but straitlaced and organized (picture *Top Gun* fighter pilots at the local bar on their day off). But make no mistake about it. When it comes to "the hunt," great salespeople have the ability to track and capture their prey with the focus and patience of a big cat.

And there is more. Driven salespeople are *never* satisfied. They can never sell enough products, never make enough money. They are insatiable, setting the bar higher and higher, for themselves and, happily, for you.

Competitiveness

Driven salespeople are hardwired to be number one. Like a Thoroughbred racehorse, they are always eyeing their peers, always comparing their performance to others. They are out to *win*. They are *born* to win.

Driven salespeople compete with everybody. Even the sale itself is seen, on one level, as a battle of wills with the buyer, a competition in which the sale signals victory.

This competitiveness is one reason great salespeople are sometimes hard to manage. They even compete, intellectually, with their bosses. But it is a trade-off that must be reconciled because competitiveness is a critical element of Drive, and without Drive, a person simply will not perform to your sales expectations.

Optimism

Optimism is the Driven salesperson's ultimate weapon. Optimism provides the body armor to withstand the inevitable rejections of the selling life. To a great salesperson, rejection is just part of the game, like grounding out in baseball. No problem, because surely the next time at bat will bring a home run.

In an interesting, psychological paradox, optimistic sales-people credit themselves for success but do not take defeat personally. Like astronauts, they have "the right stuff" when it comes to facing down fear and placing risk in a more positive context than most people are able to do.

Recognizing Drive

Need for achievement, competitiveness, and optimism— all are essential to generate the nuclear fission that sales psy-chologists refer to as Drive. Given such a powerful profile, you would think we would be able to recognize a Driven salesperson when we see one. But, in a cruel paradox for business owners and managers, *that is often not the case.* Drive is often misunderstood, and it can be faked, for a short time, leading to the waste of hundreds of thousands of dollars, if not millions, in the process. (Hint: it is often the server or the dishwasher at the local restaurant who is working to pay for college, not the campus club president, who has the Drive to succeed as a top-performing salesper-son.) In fact, in a recent study by psychology professor Murray Barrick and colleagues, a group of human resources professionals—each of whom had more than 12 years of experience—was *unable* to accurately identify whether job candidates were industrious or persistent in the face of failure. They thus failed to discern two traits (need for achievement, represented by industriousness, and optimism, represented by persistence in the face of failure) that are key elements of Drive.

So how do we recognize *real* Drive in candidates or incum-bent salespeople? How can we be sure we are not mistaking chutzpah for competitiveness, anxiety for ambition? To find out, let's take a journey together into the heart of a salesperson who is Driven—a journey into the heart of a *winner!*

Summary

◆ Research shows that Drive is the most important factor for sales success.

◆ Three elements make up Drive: (1) need for achievement, (2) competitiveness, and (3) optimism. All three elements *must* be present for the salesperson to truly show Drive.

◆ A company's performance is dependent on the quality of the salespeople it hires, necessitating a much more rigorous screening process to identify and select Driven candidates than many companies currently deploy.

Chapter

The Need to Achieve

Tibetan Sherpas tell the story that, moments after reaching the summit of Mount Everest, a climber briefly admired the view, then turned to his partner and said, "OK, now what?"

Insatiable. Never satisfied. Demanding excellence. These are powerful personality characteristics (perhaps not easy to live with, from the point of view of one's spouse or child) but absolutely critical to the profile of a highly successful salesperson.

Need for achievement is the inner motivation that causes a person to relentlessly pursue excellence. As psychology professor David McClelland and his colleagues reported in their 1987 book Human Motivation, people high in need for achievement want to do well for the *personal satisfaction* achievement brings. This intense motivation pushes people to set tough but achievable goals, to find innovative solutions, and to take personal responsibility for their performance. In other words, the prescription for a dream salesperson.

As detailed in his 1961 book *The Achieving Society*, McClelland found an association between high need for achievement and sales ability across several cultures. In particular, he noted that sales careers are attractive to achievers because salespeople must make decisions about which prospects to call on, take personal responsibility for making calls, choose moderate risks, find creative methods of persuasion, and monitor their success. Supporting McClelland's assertion, University of Memphis psychology professor Andrew Vinchur and his colleagues analyzed the results of 98 previous studies of personality factors that predict sales performance. These studies spanned the years 1918 to 1996 and included a total of about 46,000 salespeople. Vinchur's group reported in 1998 that *achievement motivation showed a stronger relationship to sales performance than any other trait.* In a 1999 study at Cornell University, a group led by Renate Soyer also noted that individuals who have a strong need for achievement are likely to thrive in sales. These researchers found that such individuals *view rejection as constructive criticism, prioritize the customer, and carefully research their competitors.*

Finally, in a 2004 study, we tested the personality traits of 89 salespeople in mixed industry sectors, including manufacturing and financial services. We compared scores on a personality test to sales managers' ratings of each person's performance. Our results supported the research literature: need for achievement was a more powerful predictor of sales performance than any other trait.

Testing Need for Achievement

McClelland and his colleagues found two interesting ways to test a person's need for achievement. First, they used the Thematic Apperception Test, which asks users to make up stories about a series of pictures. They reasoned that people's fantasies about the pictures were the best measures of their inner goals and desires. The pictures were all rather ordinary drawings. For example, they included a boy looking down at a violin with a sad expression on his face. But when psychologists looked at the subjects' responses, they found something striking.

People with a high need for achievement told very different stories than the average person. For example, after viewing the violin picture, someone with a low need for achievement would tell a story about how the boy's parents bought him this boring violin and made him practice every day. He is sick of practicing and wants to smash the violin and go outside to play. The violin is too much work to learn. However, someone with a high need for achievement would tell a story about a big recital coming up the next day for which the boy is practicing. He is dog-tired from practicing all night, but he wants to get in one more hour before dozing off. Then the following day, he gives the performance of a lifetime!

McClelland's second test to show need for achievement involved a seemingly simple experiment. He asked volunteers to throw rings onto pegs—without telling them how far back to stand. Most subjects threw from random distances. But the high achievers in the group measured the distance to produce an ideal challenge (not too easy but not impossible). Achievers love a tough task at which they can excel.

> Through his work, McClelland concluded that many people do not possess a strong need for achievement. That means we need to be expert at selecting the genuine article when it comes to salespeople.

The Birth of Desire

Where does this need to achieve come from? Like most personality traits, it is heavily influenced by a person's childhood experiences. In his 1997 book *Psychological Self-Help*, clinical psychologist Clayton Tucker-Ladd noted that achievers' parents or guardians are praising, supportive, optimistic, hardworking, and success oriented. They expect each member of the family to do a share of the chores and follow household rules. Dinner discussions are about the child's work and studies. But these achieving kids are not always star students. They excel at whatever is important to them in accomplishing their goals. If they see academics as important, they excel there. If it's a sports career they're after, they excel at athletics. Others may devote their time to entrepreneurial activities, such as running a lemonade stand or making T-shirts. This pattern continues throughout such people's lives, right up to the moment they are sitting across from your desk in the job interview. That's why using the right set of questions will help you figure out whether a candidate is the genuine article or a sloth in a tiger's clothing.

Unfortunately, there is a catch. (There's always a catch.) Even with the best questions available, it is very, very difficult to determine who has the *real*, deep *need to achieve* and who merely "acts like" they have this need. Let's take a moment here to distinguish the "pretenders" from the "producers."

Watch Out for Fakers

Some candidates in sales may make a good first impression but nevertheless lack the critical need for achievement to stay focused and productive for the long haul. We have identified several of these imposters, whom we classify as *narcissists, ultra–type A personalities,* and *flatliners.*

Narcissists

Narcissists are people with inflated egos who can *seem* to be ambitious, persuasive, and self-confident in a sales interview. However, deep down, they harbor intense insecurities which ultimately cause them to fail as salespeople. As Soyer's group pointed out, narcissists often can determine what you, as the employer, are looking for during an interview and then *mimic* the prototype. Narcissists can be incredibly charming, which you would think would

A skilled narcissist is very hard to detect without proper testing and interviewing techniques (which we will discuss in chapter 9). For now, be aware that the need to achieve is a legitimate, deep-seated trait that pushes high achievers and great salespeople over the long haul, not just during the lovefest of the interview and the hiring process, when the narcissist often stands out—for the moment.

help them succeed if hired. But their brief spurt of charm is not enough, because sales is ultimately a marathon, and the narcissist is usually a sprinter.

Ultra–Type A Personalities

While it may seem confusing on the surface, there is a critical difference between what psychologists diagnose as extreme *type A* personalities and people with a deep need to achieve. When it comes to salespeople, the distinction boils down to this: while extreme type A people can be achievement oriented, they can also be impatient, irritable, and hostile. These characteristics can lead to depression and dissatisfaction with their jobs, bosses, or clients—hardly the team orientation necessary for a company to grow and prosper as an organization.

Occasionally, a client will tell us, "We are looking for type As." As advisers, we like to recast that goal to "We are looking for A players," our criterion being a *need to achieve,* not a need to make everybody else crazy. Most of the best salespeople we know keep their emotions well under control, even as they relentlessly drive for achievement. They can be prima donnas, but they do not compromise their performance with excess collateral damage.

Flatliners

We received a call from a printer in Minneapolis. His story was all too familiar. Steve, his highest-paid salesperson, had plateaued. "I don't get it," lamented our client. "This is the third year in a row Steve has hit the same numbers. Our business is growing. We are giving him more resources. But we can't seem to light a fire under him to raise his game."

Steve is what we call a *flatliner.* Unlike the mountain climber who reached the pinnacle of Mount Everest, Steve is satisfied with the lovely view at 10,000 feet. Steve may be motivated by money but not by more than he needs to lead a peaceful life *below your expectations.* He has designed a certain lifestyle, and he earns just enough to support it.

Now, there is nothing wrong with Steve as a person. Who's to say he hasn't achieved the "balance" we are all looking for in life? *But he is not going to grow your business.* You may want to retain him as a solid contributor, but to grow, you will need to find another horse to bet on, one with the burning need to achieve.

Sales managers sometimes make a mistake in thinking that the antidote for underachievers is, ultimately, more money. But special promotions and higher commissions rarely work for flatliners. The real A players will love it, but they would have performed anyway because they are self-motivated and do not need your help.

It's Not About the Money

For the narcissists, ultra type As, and flatliners, their underperformance is not about the money. It's about their inability to sustain high-quality performance over time, under any circumstances (or compensation formulas). They will not, or cannot, apply the dedication nor make the sacrifices necessary to lift your business and your investment in them on their shoulders.

On the other hand, salespeople with a strong need for achievement want to do well for its own sake. Their primary goal is achievement, not money. To an achiever, money is like points on a scoreboard. Just as Michael Jordan was not motivated simply to score points, top salespeople are not motivated by money alone. They simply use their income to keep track of how well they are doing (assuming that their compensation is competitive with the market).

Our sales heroes, our real achievers, are born to run, not only against their own insatiable expectations but against others as well. And not only do they need to *achieve,* they *love to compete,* keep score, and win. Let's find out why and discover how to recognize this thirst for competition in our next chapter.

Summary

◆ Eighty years of research have shown *need for achievement* to be a critical component of sales success.

◆ This basic desire for personal excellence is especially important in sales, where the freedom from daily supervision can attract slackers who want a free ride.

◆ Sales careers also attract self-centered narcissists, ultra–type A personalities, and flatliners, all of whom can be charming in a sales interview. It is imperative that managers know how to weed these people out early to avoid the hemorrhaging of resources they will likely cause if hired.

3
Chapter

The Thrill of Competition

We were killing time, and I beat Michael (Jordan) in a casual game of pool. You would have thought I stole his last dollar. He made me keep playing, game after game, until he finally beat me.

—Phil Jackson

We know from our last chapter that Driven salespeople have a deep-seated need to achieve. It motivates them to train longer, try harder, and never give up when it comes to reaching their goals and objectives in life. Now comes the second piece of the puzzle: their passion for *competition.*

People with Drive love to *compete*. They relish the thrill of the race, the rush of winning, virtually anytime, anyplace. And, like Michael Jordan, they *hate* losing. In fact, their loathing for losing is often as strong as their lust for winning—a potent combination indeed.

We have all read stories about older professional athletes who attempt to make comebacks, well past their prime. Or others who attempt to take up a different sport, such as professional golf, later in their careers. These people cannot live happily without competition. The lucky ones find new and equally exciting ways to compete as they get older.

Competitiveness is Crucial

Psychologists define *competitiveness* as the desire to win and to outperform others. Competitive salespeople monitor their performance constantly to make sure they are surpassing their peers. They work hard to prepare for a task to make sure that they outperform others.

> **To a competitive salesperson, the sale is often viewed as a contest of wills with the customer. Essentially, it is a contest between the salesperson's product or service and the customer's resistance or inertia, hence the expression "winning the sale." This desire to convince others of the validity of one's opinion is also a form of competitiveness. Organizational psychologist Herbert Greenberg and his colleagues in 2001 labeled this aspect of competitiveness *ego-drive,* or an**

> **individual's desire to persuade others. They noted that this trait is crucial for success and *impossible* to teach.**

Competitiveness Research

In a 1994 paper, Geoffrey Brewer, editorial director of Gallup Press, reported a survey of a half million salespeople from companies including Federal Express, Strycker Surgical, and Home Savings of America, which concluded that competitiveness is an essential trait for sales success.

University of Memphis marketing professor Balaji Krishnan and his colleagues conducted a study to find out why competitiveness improves sales performance. They tested 182 real estate salespeople and reported in 2003 their finding that competitiveness combined with other key personality traits caused salespeople to work harder and subsequently outperform their peers.

In a 1998 study, University of Houston marketing professor Steven Brown and his colleagues tested 158 medical supplies salespeople and found that highly competitive salespeople who saw the company climate as competitive consistently set higher goals. Conversely, salespeople who were low in competitiveness consistently set lower goals, regardless of what they thought of the company climate.

Taken together, previous research shows that *competitiveness leads to greater effort and better performance in sales*. Many sales managers realize this fact but make a crucial mistake: they assume that a former athlete will make a great salesperson. That is a myth, pure and simple. Most sales managers have hired one or two former high school or college athletes who once set the gridiron or basketball court on fire with their athletic prowess. Then, months down the road, something shocking happens. These managers find out that a number of ex-athletes do not cut it as producers. What is going on here?

Competitiveness is not enough!

In reality, there is no guarantee that former athletes will be good salespeople. Remember, competitiveness is only *one* element of Drive. Although it is an essential trait, competitiveness is not enough for sales success. Top performers must also have the need for achievement we discussed in chapter 2. Need for achievement is what causes star athletes to set their sights on a championship instead of just surpassing their peers. Need for achievement is what puts superstar status in the crosshairs of top salespeople. These two factors work together to motivate what we call *Competitive Achievers*.

In our work with sales managers, we have gotten to know some extraordinary salespeople who exemplify Competitive Achievement. These people are consistently ranked above their peers and produce remarkable numbers. Our interviews with them have shown that the combination of achievement motivation and competitiveness holds the key to generating consistent, superior performance. We will briefly describe two such examples.

Case Study 1

One such sales star, Greg, was a sales representative for a large manufacturing firm. He consistently outperformed his peers and was a mentor to the newer salespeople in the position. As we were discussing his work habits, he said, "I exceed my manager's expectations by working 70 hours a week. I feel good every month when management sees my numbers. I'm motivated to please our CEO. I'm also competitive every day with Jack [the company's other top salesperson]. I beat him in two of the last three months . . . It's nice to make the money also."

Here we can see the combination of need for achievement and competitiveness delivering the necessary one-two punch. Greg sets the bar for his own accomplishments high and does whatever it takes to meet his goals. He is also constantly competing for the spot of top dog on the sales team. It is clear in Greg's record-setting track record that the combination of strong achievement motivation and competitiveness gives him the Drive to succeed.

Case Study 2

Another top salesperson with a hydraulics company, Janice, granted us some time to discuss how she consistently achieved stellar numbers and surpassed her peers. She said, "In every sale, I go in with a purpose and a focus: is my action making money or losing money? I'm very competitive. I want to know where I stand overall [compared to other sales reps]; I was *born* with Drive."

Again, here we clearly see the intense love of competition. Janice is focused on being the top salesperson in her company. Her need for achievement keeps her motivated to set performance goals much higher than those of the average rep.

Both of these top performers amaze their managers and are the envy of their peers. Both of them achieve remarkable results and reap significant rewards. And it is clear that both rely on the combination of competitiveness and need for achievement as the foundation of their success. Without these two traits, neither could attain such high levels of performance.

Fortunately, passion for competition is relatively easy to identify through the course of proper testing and interviewing. While our old friend the narcissist can *claim* to love competition, we can flush that element out with questions which put this person in a position to choose between a competitive situation and alternatives that require less risk and less reward.

It's important to remember that there is a key difference between a love for competition and simply a desire to win at all costs. The former involves the lust for a good game, the invigoration and growth that come from the

Our A and B salespeople never stop competing and consequently never stop developing. Wise business owners and sales managers feed this tempest with internal and external competitive challenges that bring out the best in their top producers and often help identify those who cannot, or will not, engage. They know that the big dogs love to keep score, relish feedback, and thrive on the thrill of the game.

competitive process itself. The latter can involve shortcuts and easy routes to a shallow victory.

At this point, we have two parts of the Drive model for high-performance salespeople in place. Let's now move to lock in the third critical element—the characteristic that pulls it all together—the top salesperson's supreme sense of self-assurance: *optimism*.

Summary

♦ Competitiveness is crucial to sales success. This finding has been proven by academic research and our extensive practice.

♦ *Competitiveness* must be combined with the *need for achievement* to create a high-performing Competitive Achiever. Such a person is motivated to achieve and loves to compete.

♦ Hiring a former athlete is no guarantee that you will have a top performer. The person must also have the *ambition* to match the desire to win.

♦ Competitiveness and need for achievement are still not enough to give a salesperson *lasting* Drive. Optimism, the third element of Drive, is also crucial.

Chapter

Optimism

Years ago, when I played high school basketball, I had the "privilege" of guarding our state's best player, a real gunner whom I "held" to 49 points. Later, we became good friends, and I asked him if he ever felt discouraged if he missed a shot. He said, "Actually, it's just the opposite. I'm around a 50 percent shooter. If I miss a shot, I can't wait to take the next one because I'm absolutely sure I'll make it."

—Richard Abraham

You would think that the combination of a burning *need to achieve* and a *love of competition* would be enough to drive our super salespeople to succeed. But even some of our Competitive Achievers won't make the cut because of a brutal anomaly: while they yearn for success, they are *terrified of failure*. They are so terrified, in fact, that fear blocks the realization of hopes and dreams that their skills could otherwise achieve.

> **Years of testing have revealed that salespeople who *expect to succeed every time* will *close* far more often than those who are afraid of the alternative. In fact, salespeople's expectations of success or failure ultimately determine whether they can unleash the full power of their natural talent. When they think about tomorrow's meeting with a key prospect, they see only the close. To them, there is no other possibility!**

This sense of certainty comes from the third and final facet of Drive: *optimism*. More than 30 years of research have shown that *optimism is a critical element for sales success*. Salespeople with optimism have two key advantages over their pessimistic peers:

1. *Optimists expect to win*. When they think about the sales call tomorrow, they *see* the close. This positive visualization sets up a self-fulfilling prophecy of success.

2. *Optimists are thick-skinned*. They don't take rejection personally. They interpret a failure as something temporary, unusual, and outside of their control. They have the constitution to put rejection in its proper perspective.

In a 1999 review of 30 years of optimism research, Peter Schulman, research director of the Martin Seligman Research Alliance, discussed the relationship between optimism and motivation. He noted that "the ability to succeed and the desire to succeed are not always enough without the belief that one *will* succeed. Someone with the talent of a Mozart can come to nothing in the absence of that belief. This is particularly true when the task at hand is challenging and requires persistence to overcome obstacles and setbacks (like sales!)."

Although optimism seems like an obvious necessity, many managers don't recognize or emphasize its importance when recruiting salespeople. Even as trained psychologists, *we* learned about the supreme importance of optimism the hard way.

Several years ago we performed a psychological evaluation on a potential salesperson for a hardware leasing company (let's call him Chuck). The interview showed that Chuck was absolutely a Competitive Achiever. He had a track record of going for the gold and for working as hard as necessary to get it. He also had other personality traits we were looking for in salespeople, so we recommended him for the position. However, after about six months, he began to bog down. Though Chuck had lofty goals and wanted to be at the top of the sales team, his sales did not match his ambitions.

We and our client were confused. How could someone who was clearly a Competitive Achiever, with such other necessary traits as persuasiveness and relationship and organizational skills, not make the grade? Something else was obviously missing—but what?

As we dug deeper, the mystery began to reveal itself. Chuck's sales manager told us that in a recent sales meeting, a reluctant prospect became the subject of conversation. Chuck thought this topic was a waste of time, saying that the prospect clearly did not want to buy because he did not understand the value of the service being offered. Chuck wanted to change the subject to bigger goals and warmer leads. But one of his peers stopped him: "Wait a minute; this is a huge opportunity to educate this customer about the value of our service. This could be a profitable client, and I'm sure we can land him." Chuck just looked perplexed.

Clearly, Chuck was motivated, but he lacked the *optimism* to keep pushing. He loved to succeed in general but just did not have the optimism necessary to succeed at the rough-and-tumble game of overcoming rejections. In the end, he felt so bad about not reaching his goals that he offered to pay the sales manager back every dollar of salary he received. Chuck's manager admired his character but did not take him up on the offer. Chuck and his company parted ways, amicably, having learned a valuable lesson.

This incident from our early days of practice caused us to research the optimism trait in depth. We learned that a salesperson can be highly motivated but lack the sense of certainty that he or she will succeed. Without optimism, Chuck and thousands like him have struggled desperately in sales careers—aiming high, wanting to do well, but unable to muster the confidence to persevere and succeed.

The Evidence for Optimism

Martin Seligman and his colleagues pioneered the study of optimism in salespeople. More than 30 years of their research with more than one million salespeople have confirmed the importance of this trait. We now understand what causes some salespeople to keep moving forward and others to crumble when they hear the word *no*. It's usually based on the way salespeople perceive and explain rejections and setbacks to themselves and others.

For example, in a 1986 study, Seligman and Schulman tested the explanatory style of life insurance agents for Metropolitan Life and compared it to their sales performance. The results showed that salespeople who habitually explained a negative event as internal ("it's my fault"), stable ("it's going to last forever"), or global ("it's going to undermine everything I do") consistently sold much less insurance than optimistic salespeople did. In fact, the optimistic salespeople sold 37 percent more insurance than their pessimistic coworkers. Unlike the pessimists, the optimists explained negative events as external ("I'm not at fault"), unstable ("this is only temporary"), and specific ("this is isolated to this one situation"). Cutting it even finer, the most optimistic salespeople of the group sold 88 percent more insurance than the most pessimistic. The researchers also found that optimists stayed on the job at twice the rate of pessimists, who were more likely to quit at great cost to their employers.

Seligman and Schulman then applied their findings to recruiting at Metropolitan Life. They tested 14,000 applicants for optimism. Applicants also completed Metropolitan Life's regular personality test, which identified applicants whose personality profiles matched current top performers. Two interesting findings emerged. First, optimists outsold pessimists by their second year; and second, *optimists even outsold the pessimists who scored higher on the regular personality test.*

Schulman went on to compare optimism scores to performance of salespeople across several industries, including office products, real estate, banking, and car sales. The results he reported in 1995 across all industries studied indicated that optimists outsold pessimists by 20 to 40 percent!

In a 1993 study, marketing professors David Strutton and James Lumpkin examined why optimists are more likely to succeed at sales. They tested the personalities of 101 salespeople from the textile manufacturing, furniture manufacturing, and communication technology industries. The findings showed that optimists and pessimists differed in how they dealt with a problem. Optimistic salespeople focused on solving the problem because they believed that the situation could change. Pessimists, on the other hand, were more likely to react by focusing on their own bad feelings and giving up. Obviously, the pessimist's reaction leads to poor performance.

Optimism is an incredibly positive characteristic in all walks of life, but it is particularly crucial to the success of a salesperson. Optimistic salespeople believe problems can be solved, so they persist. Pessimistic salespeople give up, often before the opportunity to close has been fully developed. Optimistic salespeople do not dwell on rejection. Pessimistic salespeople focus on their bad feelings, often blame themselves, or avoid the selling situation altogether to reduce stress. Optimistic salespeople feel that the next call will be a winner.

The Perfect Storm

So there we have it—the three elements of Drive: (1) the need to achieve, (2) competitiveness, and (3) optimism. Two out of three won't cut it. All must be present in the heart of the great salesperson. We have established that need for achievement and competitiveness combine to create what we know as *Competitive Achievement*. We have also made it clear that all the motivation in the world won't carry the day if a salesperson lacks optimism. Optimism is the third force that gives us real *Drive*.

As one psychologist puts it, "if need for achievement is the engine, and competitiveness is the steering wheel, optimism is the key to the engine. Without it, you're never getting out of the garage."

The Four Types

The following model provides an interesting snapshot of the relationship between Competitive Achievement and optimism in salespeople. We will describe each of the four types of salespeople categorized by this model, only one of which you would actually want to hire.

High	Quitter	Star
Low	Lazy	Hopeful

Competitive Achievement

Optimism *High*

Lazy

This type results from the combination of *low Competitive Achievement and low optimism*. These people are pretty easy to identify. They are content with limited performance and doubt their ability to succeed. Lazy salespeople give you headaches with their inaction. They put off prospecting and are slow to respond to customer requests. It is nearly impossible to change these people. They'll show brief flashes of effort when they think their job is threatened, but then they'll fall back into their old patterns.

Hopeful

This type results from the combination of *low Competitive Achievement and high optimism*. These people will do little to follow up with prospects, but expect that they will call any day. They are often very sociable and will bring customers a pizza, chat for a few hours, and leave without asking for the order. If you confront them, they will insist that things are going to improve any day. The Hopeful salesperson is often cheerful and fun to be around. Customers probably like this person as well. (Who doesn't like free pizza or doughnuts now and then?) Several years ago, a sales manager we worked with fired a Hopeful salesperson only to receive calls from customers saying how much they had liked him! Of course they liked him—he never pressed them for an order.

A word of caution. The Hopeful types are likely to stick around forever unless you make a move. In their 1986 study, Seligman and Schulman found that low producers who were high in optimism remained in their positions significantly longer than those low in optimism.

Be careful of Hopeful types in job interviews! They often come highly recommended by customers. We recently conducted a candidate assessment and found that the candidate lacked motivation but was brimming with optimism. When we called the hiring manager to make our recommendation, the manager was shocked that we were not recommending the candidate. "But he got such rave reviews from his customers," the manager protested. "Exactly," we replied, "and *your* customers would love him too." But the name of the game is not likability, it's production, and that inevitably requires exerting some pressure on the customers to close the sale.

Quitter

This type results from the combination of *high Competitive Achievement and low optimism.* Also attractive interviewers, these people initially are brimming with ambition and competitiveness, and they sound ready to light the world on fire. However, Quitters get discouraged after they experience repeated rejections. The more rejection involved in the job, the sooner they will quit.

Star

This type has the winning combination: *high Competitive Achievement and high optimism.* These people are our sales heroes. They are our top performers. Stars work hard to establish new accounts and strengthen current relationships. They love the thrill of getting new business. They are full of ambition and certain of victory.

Where do *your* salespeople fit in this model? If your company is like most, you will have a scattered diagram ranging from a handful of real Stars to a slew of salespeople you intuitively know are Hopeful, or Lazy, or even Quitters.

Fasten your seatbelt or knock back a stiff shot of bourbon before you read the next chapter because we are going to help you calculate how much it's costing you to carry people who are not Stars in the top right quadrant, people not born to sell. But don't get too discouraged. We will spend the rest of the book working with you to identify, recruit, and motivate real producers—the only type that deserves to be representing your interests in the marketplace.

Summary

- ◆ Optimism is an essential component of Drive, a trait that turns Competitive Achievers into closers.

- ◆ Optimistic Competitive Achievers have two key advantages:

  1. They set up a self-fulfilling prophecy of success.

  2. They have a thick skin and thus bounce back quickly from rejection.

- ◆ Research evidence has shown that optimists consistently outsell pessimists.

- ◆ Competitive Achievement and optimism combine in certain ways to make up four common types of salespeople.

  1. *Lazy* salespeople are low in both Competitive Achievement and optimism.

  2. *Hopeful* salespeople are low in Competitive Achievement but high in optimism.

  3. *Quitters* are high in Competitive Achievement but low in optimism.

  4. *Stars* are high in both Competitive Achievement and optimism.

Chapter 5

The High Cost of Low Performance

Rule No. 1: Never lose money.
Rule No. 2: Never forget Rule No. 1.

—Warren Buffett

It never ceases to amaze us, as business investors and advisers, when we encounter the astonishing difference between a company's zero tolerance attitude regarding the performance of, say, a $500,000 piece of machinery it has purchased and its passive response regarding a mediocre salesperson who burns $200,000 to $300,000 *per year* in opportunity and carrying costs. When we point this out to the owner-manager, we invariably get a response like, "It doesn't cost us *that* much."

Unfortunately, it *does* cost that much—and more—to train, manage, coddle, support, and carry underperformers, not to mention opportunity costs and the psychological toxins that such people spread throughout the organization.

Most sales teams have three kinds of salespeople:

- ◆ A players—those in the top 10 percent of talent available for the position

- ◆ B players—definitely keepers, but require some development

- ◆ C players—those who should not have been hired

We will discuss these distinctions more when we talk about upgrading your current team. But before we can go any further, we need to understand the outrageous cost of *tolerating sales mediocrity*. We have therefore prepared some simple calculations we would like you to do along with us.

The Cost Calculator

Step 1: First, write down the annual revenue you expect out of an A player. Please pencil in your answer right here on line 1.

1. _____

Step 2: Next, write on line 2 how much revenue one of your marginal C players generates each year. To give you some guidance, we usually expect that C players will deliver about 50 percent of what A players produce.

2. _____

Step 3: Subtract line 2 from line 1 and write the result on line 3. This difference is your annual *revenue gap for each* C player.

3. _____

Step 4: Now let's analyze the more insidious costs each C player lays on your company. First, think about the number of customers a C player loses through neglect, misbehavior, or both. What does *that* cost you annually? We know it's nearly impossible to estimate quickly. For purposes of this discussion, let's be conservative. Figure one lost customer per year, or 10 percent of an A player's revenue. Write that figure on line 4.

4. _____

Step 5: Next, consider the amount of extra time that you or your sales manager spend coaching C players. They certainly need a lot more help than your best players. For example, you probably have to spend extra time holding their hand preparing for a presentation to a major prospect. Or, you may need to have a candid conversation with them after they blow an important pitch. How about helping them get organized so they get to their territory on time?

A 2004 study by consulting firms the Future Foundation and SHL showed that the typical manager in the United States spends 13 percent of his or her time each week managing underperformers. In fact, the authors of the study estimated the total annual cost of managing underperformers in the United States at *$105.5 billion.*

To figure the cost of *your* time and a C player's slow learning curve, we typically use 25 percent of a C player's annual salary as an index for extra coaching. Write that figure on line 5.

5. _____

Step 6: Now add up lines 3, 4, and 5 and write the result on line 6. This is your *total loss in annual revenue per C player.*

6. _____

Step 7: Gross profit is probably the most accurate way to determine the carnage caused by poor salespeople. To calculate your annual loss, let's consider your loss in gross profit per C player. Simply multiply line 6 by your gross profit margin and write the result on line 7. For example, if your total loss in annual revenue on line 6 is $600,000, and your gross profit margin is 20 percent, your annual loss is $120,000.

7. _____

At this point, you may be surprised how much poor or mediocre salespeople are costing you. But, make no mistake: research shows that *hiring problems in sales are as costly as, if not more expensive than, bad hires at the senior executive level.*

Now comes perhaps the most damaging element of all: *the cost of delaying action.* We are all guilty of putting off unpleasant confrontations, hoping the situation will somehow right itself on its own. Unfortunately, if a salesperson is not high in Drive—that is, if the salesperson is a C player—research shows that the situation won't improve, and every month that goes by is a serious hemorrhage of the company's resources. Let's continue.

Step 8: Line 7 already shows you what it will cost to wait another year; copy that figure on line 8b. You can easily multiply the figure by 2 or 3 to see how much waiting *two or three years* will cost; write the results of those calculations on lines 8c and 8d. Even a six-month delay in action can be costly; divide line 8b by 2 and write the result on line 8a. Now, take a few minutes to let these costs sink in. We'll wait for you to return from the liquor cabinet.

8a. Cost of waiting six months: _____

8b. Cost of waiting one year: _____

8c. Cost of waiting two years: _____

8d. Cost of waiting three years: _____

> **The bottom line: Underperformers—C players— can kill your business.**

Why Won't They Perform?

Why won't they perform? In 1992, marketing professor Thomas Ingram and his colleagues surveyed 126 owner-managers about the factors that contribute to sales failure. Their conclusions: (1) poor listening skills; (2) failure to concentrate on top priorities; (3) lack of sufficient effort; (4) inability to determine customer needs; (5) lack of preparation for sales presentations; (6) inadequate knowledge of the product or service. What do *all* of these elements have in common? They all relate to a lack of Drive.

We can't tell you how many times we have been called into companies by desperate owner-managers who say, "Fix my sales team" or "Train my people to perform." When we arrive, we are introduced to a group of salespeople who would rather be somewhere else (the A and B players want to be out selling, the C players want to find somewhere to hide).

We go around the table and ask the salespeople to tell us a little bit about themselves as we compare each person with his or her production numbers. We always wait until our testing and interviewing have been completed to reach our final conclusions. However, all too often, it is obvious within *fifteen minutes* that *half* the people in the room shouldn't be there in the first place. They certainly should not be soaking up precious executive time and training dollars.

But here's the real kicker, the scenario that literally drives us crazy as business advisers and investors in our own right: when we bring our findings to owner-managers, we often receive responses like, "Try to train them anyway" or "Well, I need *someone* out there selling for me." Then, there's the classic, "I don't have the time or the money to go through a rigorous assessment process."

Since investing in hiring salespeople *who can actually sell* is a virtual no-brainer and easily represents the biggest bang for the business owner's buck, these kinds of questions usually reflect deeper management issues that go beyond the scope of this book. Our job, in this context, is to help owners understand that if they really want to improve their sales force and raise revenues, they should not waste money on trying to train lost causes. Train the true salespeople, redeploy the others, and backfill or recruit with the rigor that the stakes demand. When it comes to hiring new salespeople, you must recruit players with Drive and discontinue investing in salespeople who will let you down. How can you determine the difference? We begin to show you in chapter 6. We will give you a strategy for handling your current salespeople in chapter 10.

Summary

- ◆ Underperforming C players typically cost companies tens to hundreds of thousands of dollars in revenue annually.

- ◆ Most sales teams have at least a few C players on board.

- ◆ It is critical for a responsible sales manager to learn how much they are losing in annual revenues due to C players.

- ◆ Sales managers must take action on underperformers who lack Drive and replace them with A players.

Part Two:

Hiring Drivers

Testing: The First Step

At this point in our journey, we have come to appreciate the importance of Drive as the key personality characteristic that is hardwired in successful salespeople. We now know that Drive is made up of three elements: need for achievement; competitiveness; and optimism. Each of these elements is essential for high sales performance. We have also calculated the cost of carrying low-Drive players. This is often the largest area of financial loss, but it is also the richest opportunity for improvement in any business enterprise.

Now we turn to the solution—the formula, if you will, for identifying, hiring, and retaining A and B salespeople— salespeople who are born to run and who have the ability to meet and exceed your highest expectations.

A quick word of caution: this process requires patience and discipline. It is always tempting to give in to our gut instincts, to try to save time (and work) by substituting intuition for process. But 80 years of research and *billions* of wasted dollars tell us to take the time and make the effort to fill these critical positions with people who have the potential to succeed—people who are Driven to sell.

Two Steps to Hiring Drivers

There are two steps to hiring Drivers: *screening* and *interviewing*. The first step weeds out low-potential candidates, directing our time and resources toward interviewing only the cream of the crop—the potential pros.

When it's done well, this process is not unlike the National Football League's Annual Testing Combine in Indianapolis. The Combine is the process by which NFL head coaches and general managers assess the upcoming talent pool that is leaving college each year. Attendance at the Combine is by invitation only. Athletes who attend go through a series of rigorous physical and mental tests. These challenges include the 40-yard dash, bench press, vertical jump, and, yes, psychological tests and interviews. When the process is finished, owners can be confident that they have some real talent on their hands: someone who can run fast and jump high; someone who is worth their time to assess further, face-to-face, through an interview. Team officials use the results of these tests to evaluate the talent pool and make their final draft picks. Usually, those who perform well at the Combine get drafted in the early rounds. Players who don't perform well at the Combine may not get drafted at all.

Like the NFL, top business organizations often use a rigorous process to select talent. To begin, these companies use validated tests to help screen candidates, narrowing down the applicant pool to those who have true potential. Then, similar to the Combine, those who make it past this first hurdle move on to the second hurdle: rigorous interviews with the hiring manager(s) and human resource professionals. Finally, those who make it past this second hurdle move on to the final step, an interview with a psychologist to conclusively validate their potential and decide how best to manage and motivate them as they come on board.

The SalesDrive model we have created features a similar process to select sales talent. First, we test and screen out candidates with limited potential. Next, we invite serious candidates to interview with the company. Finalists make it to the most important and rigorous step in the process: the psychological interview. Let's start with the screening test in this chapter, and then we will turn to the interview process in chapters 7, 8, and 9.

Testing and Screening for Driven Salespeople

Human Resource Directors have been using personality tests for years to try to match people's personalities and aptitudes with the performance expected of them. These tests are important tools and should always be used in the context of a balanced package of assessment techniques, including résumé screening. However, they can be particularly valuable for saving time and money by providing a basic qualifier for sales candidates before bringing them in for additional assessment.

Step 1, therefore, in the recruitment of A and B salespeople, is to require each candidate to take a personality or aptitude test in order to be sure they have enough positive ingredients to warrant the interview and rigorous assessment process to follow.

Now, there are a host of credible personality tests available on the market. However, when it comes to testing specifically for Drive, we recommend a test that measures the three key Drive elements: need for achievement; competitiveness; and optimism.

EEOC Requirements

When using any type of personality test, we must keep in mind the federal government's Equal Employment Opportunity Commission (EEOC) requirements for appropriate use. These guidelines prohibit discrimination on the basis of race, creed, color, religion, gender, national origin, age (over 40), and disability. EEOC requirements also stipulate that any test used for hiring must be reliable and valid for the position in question. Here's a quick primer:

Reliability simply refers to how well a test holds up over time. In other words, will Candidate X get the same score in two weeks as was received today? Of course, the answer should be yes. Look for reliability standards in the manual supporting a given test, or ask the testing service specifically to provide reliability documentation.

> **SalesDrive features the *DriveTest* to specifically focus on Drive characteristics. Ask your testing agency how it defines and emphasizes "drive" in its testing platform.**

Validity refers to whether the test really measures what it is supposed to measure. In other words, a test of optimism should measure optimism, not anxiety or depression. The test should also predict performance in the position. That is, it *must* be relevant to the job.

Be sure to ask your testing company to provide evidence that a test is both reliable and valid. Also, be sure you have worked with HR to define the skills essential for the position (We will give you a process to do this in Chapter 8.) Finally, make certain that the test validly predicts performance in those skills at your company.

The DriveTest

SalesDrive has taken the initial testing of salespeople several steps further by developing an online test that is validated and heavily weighted, in terms of both the questions and our analysis of the answers, for identifying Drive for sales positions. While there are a number of other characteristics we look for, we think Drive is so critical that we have designed our process to emphasize this key trait.

> The architecture of the DriveTest is designed with algorithms that distinguish between people who *can* sell and people who *will* sell. This key distinction is often the place where we are able to head off flashes in the pan and people who may have the brains but not the heart to succeed as a salesperson.

Before administering the test, the hiring company must discuss the position with us to determine the necessary level of each trait measured by the test. Then candidates are invited to take the test. The following is an example of two reports generated by our psychologists indicating the test results of two candidates, one who failed and one who passed the initial DriveTest. Let's look at the weak candidate first.

Profile Report 1: Weak Candidate

Key

1 - Poor Fit	2 - Weak Fit	3 - Average Fit	4 - Good Fit	5 - Excellent Fit

Core Skill	Skill Definition	Fit				
Drive	Needs to achieve. Is ambitious. Pushes to limits of their abilities. Prepared to work long and hard in the pursuit of excellence and promotion. Needs to compete and win. Expects success. Works until the job is done.	1	2	3	4	5
Confidence	Is unfazed by rejection. Not easily offended. Will persist despite setbacks. Feels self-assured. Freely expresses opinions or concerns.	1	2	3	4	5
Persuasion	Builds a good case, taking customer needs into account. Closes compellingly. Enjoys selling and winning people over to their point of view. Stays calm under pressure.	1	2	3	4	5
Relationship	Easily establishes and maintains relationships with prospects and customers. Likes to be around people. Comfortable at social events.	1	2	3	4	5
Organization	Is disciplined and methodical. Focuses on detail. Works to keep paperwork in order. Checks thoroughly to avoid mistakes. Tracks opportunities and contacts. Task-oriented. Follows up.	1	2	3	4	5

Sales Role	Definition	Fit				
Hunter	Develops leads and new business opportunities. Closes new accounts. Fearless. Expects to win.	1	2	3	4	5
Farmer	Develops and resells existing opportunities. Follows up diligently. Grows business steadily.	1	2	3	4	5

Testing Consistency	The candidate responded consistently across the questionnaire, showing appropriate motivation and understanding of the items.

Interpretation

If Fit is Green: This salesperson shows potential to perform well in most sales positions. You should verify this potential with reference checks and in-depth interviews.

If Fit is Yellow: This salesperson has one or more aspects of their personality that could compromise sales performance. You should carefully probe low-fit areas with thorough reference checks and interviews. A professional assessment may be necessary.

If Fit is Red: This salesperson is likely to perform below standards in most sales positions.

By way of explanation, the skill definitions are standard and stay the same in each report. The Fit score ranged from 1 (Poor Fit) to 5 (Excellent Fit).

As we can quickly see from the first test, this is the type of candidate that might slide through and interview if we didn't screen such people out first. Candidates who score like this are sociable and friendly, and they have some excellent work habits. They could easily receive some nice references from people who like them. In fact, in a support capacity, they could make excellent employees.

But such a candidate is <u>not</u> a Driven salesperson.

People like this will *not* push themselves past their limits. They will *not* take rejection well. They will *not* elevate your business to the next level, for they lack the Drive to do it.

That is why a good initial test is absolutely critical. For a couple of hundred dollars, we have just saved our company thousands of dollars in additional assessment costs and interview time as well as hundreds of thousands of dollars in lost revenues from underproduction if a candidate like this one were to slide through a weak hiring process and join the company.

Now let's look at the profile of a Driven salesperson who has taken the DriveTest.

SALESDRIVE
THE SCIENCE OF SELECTING TOP PERFORMERS

Profile Report 2: Strong Candidate

Key

1 - Poor Fit	2 - Weak Fit	3 - Average Fit	4 - Good Fit	5 - Excellent Fit

Core Skill	Skill Definition	Fit				
Drive	Needs to achieve. Is ambitious. Pushes to limits of their abilities. Prepared to work long and hard in the pursuit of excellence and promotion. Needs to compete and win. Expects success. Works until the job is done.	1	2	3	4	5
Confidence	Is unfazed by rejection. Not easily offended. Will persist despite setbacks. Feels self-assured. Freely expresses opinions or concerns.	1	2	3	4	5
Persuasion	Builds a good case, taking customer needs into account. Closes compellingly. Enjoys selling and winning people over to their point of view. Stays calm under pressure.	1	2	3	4	5
Relationship	Easily establishes and maintains relationships with prospects and customers. Likes to be around people. Comfortable at social events.	1	2	3	4	5
Organization	Is disciplined and methodical. Focuses on detail. Works to keep paperwork in order. Checks thoroughly to avoid mistakes. Tracks opportunities and contacts. Task-oriented. Follows up.	1	2	3	4	5

Sales Role	Definition	Fit				
Hunter	Develops leads and new business opportunities. Closes new accounts. Fearless. Expects to win.	1	2	3	4	5
Farmer	Develops and resells existing opportunities. Follows up diligently. Grows business steadily.	1	2	3	4	5

Testing Consistency	The candidate responded consistently across the questionnaire, showing appropriate motivation and understanding of the items.

Interpretation

If Fit is Green: This salesperson shows potential to perform well in most sales positions. You should verify this potential with reference checks and in-depth interviews.

If Fit is Yellow: This salesperson has one or more aspects of their personality that could compromise sales performance. You should carefully probe low-fit areas with thorough reference checks and interviews. A professional assessment may be necessary.

If Fit is Red: This salesperson is likely to perform below standards in most sales positions.

This candidate clearly has the potential to be an A player. The person scored high on Drive as well as the other core sales skills. The candidate has potential in both account acquisition and development. If presented with two candidates like those shown in these examples, we now have powerful data to use in conjunction with our regular résumé screening process.

What are the chances that someone who is not Driven will make it through this first filter? The good news: our research shows that personality testing is around 70 percent effective in weeding out non-Drivers. The bad news: up to 30 percent can make it through if they are crafty test takers. In fact, a 2005 study by management professor Chad Van Iddekinge and his colleagues indicates that personality tests can be easier to fake than a good interview. So, we have more work to do before selecting our winners.

Still, 70 percent is a strong initial filter, and if you are not currently testing, an initial test can put you in a much better recruiting position than you are now. But research by organizational psychology professor Joe Cortina and his colleagues in 2000 has shown that a structured interview adds significantly more predictive power than testing alone. Therefore, based upon the enormous stakes and the huge cost of hiring the wrong person to carry your company's flag, *we never recommend personality or aptitude testing alone as the answer to hiring Driven salespeople.*

Passing the initial test is the first hurdle. The real game is about to begin. But before we leave the initial test, let's address a few frequently asked questions about testing:

- *Why bother using a test to screen candidates?* A screening test allows you to save valuable time and money by eliminating candidates who are clearly inappropriate for the position and shouldn't soak up precious interviewing time.

■ *What if a candidate has great references? Should I bother with the process?* Many sales managers have asked this question, especially if they know the references personally and/or need to fill the position fast. However, you should never base your hiring decision on recommendations alone, no matter the source. Those referenced may not know enough about the position at your company to make an informed recommendation. They just know they like the candidate and want the person to do well. You need to conduct a thorough assessment to make sure the candidate is truly a good fit.

■ *Can I use the initial test alone?* Screening tests are most valuable in determining candidates who are *inappropriate* for the position. They carry nowhere near the power of a full interview. Clever candidates will have a much easier time faking a test than pulling the wool over an experienced interviewer's eyes. In fact, as mentioned earlier, research has shown that a personality test is more susceptible to faking than a structured interview.

Remember, personality or aptitude testing is the essential *first step* in identifying people with Drive from within your candidate pool. Once you have qualified your finalists through the testing process, its time to engage in one of the most important processes in the lives of both your candidate and your company: the interview—an art and a science we will take you through in the next chapter.

Summary

◆ There are two steps to hiring Drivers:

1. Testing to screen out clearly inappropriate candidates, and

2. Interviewing those who pass the initial screening test.

◆ The initial screening test narrows the candidate pool and identifies candidates who have the strongest potential.

◆ The screening test must be valid, reliable, and job-relevant, and it must not discriminate against any protected group.

◆ Select a test that measures all three elements of Drive—need for achievement, competitiveness, and optimism—as well as other skills essential for the position.

◆ Passing the test is only the first hurdle for the candidate. The rigorous interview process follows for those who show potential.

7
Chapter

The Rules of Interview Engagement

My greatest strength . . . is to be ignorant and ask a few questions.

—Peter Drucker

We have discussed the enormous stakes involved in selecting the right (or wrong) people to represent our companies in the marketplace. We know that salespeople can literally make or break our businesses.

> **It is therefore astonishing to us how little precision many companies bring to the process—how often they rely on intuition, or "gut feelings," rather than leveraging the powerful information now available on the psychology of top performers. NFL teams would never bet millions of dollars on draft choices who did not have the basic skills to succeed. Why should we?**

We thus come now to the most important part of the salesperson assessment process: the face-to-face interview. This stage of the process is where we conclude whether a candidate or employee has the psychological characteristics and the intellectual aptitude to succeed in the ferociously competitive environment of sales.

Three Levels of Interviewing Horsepower

There are three levels of interviewing horsepower that organizations can apply in selecting Driven salespeople: (1) industrial psychologists, (2) formally trained assessment professionals, and (3) sales managers or business owners alone. We'll discuss them in order, from greatest to least horsepower.

1. Industrial Psychologists

Industrial psychologists are professionals who are trained to understand the behavioral patterns of people within the context of business. They are particularly skilled at digging into a candidate's work history to identify hidden behavior patterns that can slip by most other interviewers. These traits often end up making or breaking the candidate's ultimate job performance.

Companies often use organizational psychologists to interview top executives, a practice we strongly endorse. However, in a puzzling anomaly, companies usually do not expose salespeople to the same rigor, even though the opportunity or cost involved in selecting the right people to sell is arguably the most important personnel decision in the company, relating directly to top-line revenue growth.

Thus, the most successful interview platform involves an industrial psychologist who can verify the Drive personality profile in sales candidates through a rigorous, face-to-face interview.

At SalesDrive, our psychologists have developed a proprietary interview platform heavily weighted to identify Drive. The interview is conducted in person, takes about two hours, and is enormously effective in separating real Drivers from pretenders.

The SalesDrive interview itself is really the "tip of the spear" of a much more complex process. Prior to ever meeting a candidate, the psychologist conducts extensive company research and speaks to senior management to thoroughly understand the salesperson's role and the skills essential for the job. The psychologist also interviews existing A players to learn why they are succeeding in this specific environment (both internal and external) so that the candidate's interview can be tailored to real-world battle conditions.

Those candidates who make it past the DriveTest *and* the company interview with the hiring manager move on to the full Drive Interview. Once this assessment interview is completed, both the candidate and the owner or manager are consulted relative to strengths, development needs, and specific steps for improvement.

Perhaps most important, owners and managers are counseled on how best to motivate this unique person—whether the person is motivated by benevolent mentorship, for example, or occasional, tough feedback; what turns this person on or off as a human being.

The SalesDrive success rate for identifying and selecting people who not only *can* sell but *will* sell, is better than 90 percent, based on rigorous follow-up with clients at intervals of six months, one year, and two years after hiring. If you think, for a moment, about your own turnover rate, you can begin to see what kind of impact this level of assessment can have on saving the organization an incredible amount of time and money, especially over a 10-year period.

We obviously have a vested interest in SalesDrive and believe strongly in its heavy emphasis on Drive. But the overriding point here is that industrial psychologists bring a level of knowledge and insight to the assessment process that can dramatically raise a company's odds of selecting top performers.

2. Formally Trained Assessment Professionals

Some companies decide to train their own business managers or human resource (HR) managers to conduct professional-grade interviews. This qualification is accomplished by bringing in experts who conduct interview training for these managers.

This approach can be a practical alternative, particularly if there is huge scale involved. However, its success is highly dependent on the quality of the training and the aptitude of the trainers. SalesDrive and other assessment companies will license or train internal staff who can become very good interviewers. But, candidly, it is simply tough to match the experience and knowledge of a psychologist when it comes to building a team of sales stars. Even interviewers with substantial experience can find it challenging to identify Drive. For example, as we mentioned in chapter 1, one recent study showed that 26 experienced human resource professionals were unable to accurately determine whether a group of mock candidates were really industrious or persistent.

3. Sales Managers or Business Owners

Many small to midsize companies rely on sales managers, or on the business owners alone, to interview and select sales talent. We do not endorse this approach because personality assessment is complex and requires specific, psychological training to analyze. Sales managers and business owners should interview candidates for their technical skills and their fit with company culture. We do not recommend that they make final decisions regarding candidate personality traits. Nevertheless, we know that many people who read this book are hoping to receive some interviewing ideas that they can apply themselves. So, we provide here a discussion of some of our best techniques to help anyone who is trying to size up a candidate for Drive.

Five Classic Errors

First of all, it is important to recognize what *not* to do in an interview—that is, common mistakes interviewers make or traps they can fall into which lead to bad decisions. See if you recognize any of the following five classic errors.

1. The BS Session

Most business owners and sales managers we know are not short on ego, and many feel they have a "golden gut" when it comes to people. So, instead of leveraging 80 years of technical research on what makes top performers tick and using a structured set of questions, they fall back on a classic BS session as a means of sizing up the candidate.

This is a common practice among many owners or mangers who have had no formal interview training. First they talk about the position for awhile. Then they spend the rest of the time casually chatting with the candidate, trying to get a "gut feel" for him or her. They often tell us that they can "just tell" whether the candidate will make a good salesperson. *Unfortunately, "gut feelings" have cost companies millions in lost sales, missed opportunities, and lost customers.*

Now, small talk is extremely important for establishing initial rapport with the candidate. We should spend about five to 10 minutes chatting generally at the beginning. We can also pepper in a bit more of this relaxed conversation during breaks. But any more than that and we are exposing ourselves—and our companies—to much greater risk than we may realize.

Here's the problem with unstructured interviews: anyone who wants a sales job can go to the bookstore and buy one of dozens of interview guides filled with typical questions and how to prepare for them. These books advise candidates on what to wear, how to act, and specifically how to respond to "gut feeling" types of questions. Candidates also are coached to take control of the interview if possible.

Remember our friend the narcissist? If we do not conduct a structured interview, here is what these types of charming candidates will do. They will cut loose with a prepared speech about how motivated they are to sell and how excited they are to work for us. The more we eat it up, the more they will dish it out, and they will keep right on spoon-feeding us whatever we want to hear until we've got that nice "gut feeling." (Months later, we will be wondering why our gut feeling has turned to indigestion when such promising candidates fail to live up to our expectations.)

University of Iowa management professor Murray Barrick and his colleagues studied the behavior of 73 candidates who held mock interviews with experienced human resource professionals. The results they reported in 2000 showed that applicants *actively managed* the impressions they created during the interview. They presented themselves as hardworking, persistent, and dependable.

Obviously, if we are not ready with our own, structured plan, we need to be prepared to risk $150,000 on a nonproducer. To avoid being seduced, the focus *must be* on the candidate's work history. We will get into a specific recipe for this technique in a moment.

2. The "What if?" Trap

Many sales managers avoid BS but still fall victim to classic mistake number 2: the "What If?" trap. This happens when they spend too much time asking the candidate, "What would you do if . . . [for example, an irate customer called; or a customer wanted to haggle; or your hair caught on fire]?"

These are called *situational questions*. They ask the candidate how he or she would handle *hypothetical* situations on the job. Such questions can be valuable for getting a candidate's philosophies on important topics. They work well in interviews for management or administrative staff.

However, when we are interviewing a sales candidate, situational questions can get us into trouble. Essentially, they make it easier for a candidate to look good by giving away easy clues about what we want to hear. As we mentioned earlier, numerous interviewing guides are filled with these types of questions—along with their "ideal" answers.

Savvy candidates often will have their answers to these philosophical questions well prepared, but their great answers may have little or nothing to do with what they *will actually do* on the job. Through situational questions, we discuss concepts rather than performance. It's easy to agree that we both *want* candidates to succeed. But *can* they? *Will* they? For *us*!?!

The best way to predict a person's future behavior is to carefully examine what that person did in the past. Studies comparing both types of questions (such as those reported by Pulakos and Schmitt in 1995 and Huffcut and colleagues in 2001) have shown that interviews based on previous behavior are more predictive than those based on hypothetical situations. So, instead of falling into the "What if?" trap, we should use situational questions sparingly and instead focus most of our time on requests for information about a candidate's experience, for example, "Tell me about a time when you wish you had been more persuasive" or "Describe the most profitable sale you ever made." *Previous behavior is the evidence we need to support our conclusions about the candidate's ability to succeed going forward.*

3. Weak Sales Resistance

Many sales managers are former salespeople, and salespeople love to be sold! It's in the blood of every great salesperson to enjoy being persuaded. However, if we do not verify that our candidate has staying power, our love of a good sale can cost us dearly down the road.

Sales managers with weak resistance typically love it when the candidate uses traditional sales tactics in the interview. For example, if the candidate *probes for pain* by asking tough questions about the manager's real needs and then tailors his or her subsequent speech accordingly, some sales managers feel the candidate has great empathy. Similarly, when a candidate *asks for the sale* by asking for the job, the manager assumes the candidate is a solid closer. The only problem with this approach is that most semiexperienced salespeople know how to use these basic tactics. But the question is not whether they *can* sell, it's whether they *will*.

Remember, as we established earlier, job applicants are carefully managing the impressions they are trying to make on us. Often, the behavior we see on interview day may be the best sales job we ever get out of a particular candidate. So, if you like to be sold, be careful. The candidate may have just sold you on a $150,000 ride to the poorhouse.

4. Hiring Someone Like You

While we're at it, another classic interviewing mistake is hiring someone who is *just like you*. We all have a natural preference for people who seem to share our values and opinions. Although this bias is helpful for making friends, it can be terrible for hiring. When you recognize that a candidate somehow reminds you of yourself, you often are blinded to that person's negative traits. When this happens, an interviewer will typically emphasize the strengths but ignore important shortcomings that the candidate has in common with him or her.

Here's a way to avoid this problem as you interview. During a break in the interview process, you should stop and ask yourself, "How is this candidate like *me*? What do I like most about this person? What kinds of things could I be missing because of it?" (Hint: think about your *own* shortcomings.) We need to be as critical as necessary to uncover all potential weaknesses.

5. Settling for a Warm Body

Many times along your path, you will be tempted to stop and settle for a candidate who has substantial experience, simply looks the part, or "just feels right." Giving up and taking whoever is in front of you will feel so much easier, temporarily, than holding out for a real Driver.

These situations are simply tests of your resolve. They will *test* you to determine whether you really have the stamina to hire stars. Every time you pass such a test, you come one step closer to creating your dream team. Every time you give in and hire a warm body to fill a vacancy, you will be punished by failure.

We know there can be tremendous pressure to fill a vacancy, especially in a busy territory. However, business owners and sales managers who settle for nothing less than Drivers always surpass those who give in to gut instinct or nepotism. Apply the lessons in this book *patiently* and you will assemble a team capable of exceeding your expectations.

Now that we've reviewed these five classic errors, let's go on to the next chapter and examine some of the best questions to ask to find real Drivers.

Summary

- There are three levels of interviewing horsepower that organizations can apply in selecting Driven salespeople:

  1. *Organizational Psychologists.* The most successful interview platform available. They are trained at assessing deep personality traits in a job interview and finding weaknesses hidden beneath a candidate's positive facade.

  2. *Formally Trained Assessment Professionals.* HR or sales managers who have received formal interview training. Accuracy is dependent on quality of the training and skill of the trainers.

  3. *Sales Managers or Business Owners Alone.* Depends on the skill of the individual. Highly susceptible to subjective bias and "gut feeling." Recommend supplementing with technical tools.

- There are five classic errors commonly committed by most sales interviewers:

  1. *The BS Session.* Allowing the conversation to drift wherever the candidate leads you.

  2. *The "What If" Trap.* Overuse of questions asking about hypothetical situations with a sales candidate.

3. *Weak Sales Resistance.* Falling for a candidate who simply uses classic sales techniques on us in the interview.

4. *Hiring Someone Like You.* Bringing people on board just because they are a lot like you. Remember, they probably also have your shortcomings.

5. *Settling for a Warm Body.* Caving in to the pressure to hire someone just because you have a vacancy. By doing so, you risk hiring an underperformer. You will wish you held out for a Driver.

The Drive Interview

A prudent question is one half of wisdom.

—Francis Bacon

The *Drive Interview* is a proprietary, two-hour interview conducted by an industrial psychologist. It requires intense *due diligence*—that is, thorough research and analysis—to understand both the company's culture and the specific requirements of the position. The process results in an in-depth report of the candidate's strengths, areas for improvement, and suggestions for mentoring and motivating the candidate. The success rate of this process has, in our experience, been better than 90 percent.

Why is this process so successful, and what can you learn from it to help elevate your own interview skills? This chapter presents some key elements of the process, including questions we love to ask when searching for the rocket fuel we call Drive.

At SalesDrive, we follow a formula that we have labeled the *3 Ps* for ease of memory: (1) *Planning*, (2) *Probing the Past*, and (3) *Patterns*.

Planning

Planning is a process that involves two steps: defining the job requirements and preparing for the interview.

Step 1

Step 1 relates to understanding the specific requirements of the sales job in question. To determine these requirements, we first meet with management to conduct a job analysis, developing a list of the knowledge, skills, and abilities essential for the position. This initial due diligence has two parts.

1. Defining the Roles the Salesperson Plays

First, the sales manager defines the *type* of selling that is unique to the industry or the company's strategy—that is, the *roles* the salesperson plays. In the following chart, 12 aspects of the job are defined, grouped as contrasting pairs. You can use the chart to check those roles that are most relevant. In some cases you might check both items in a pair.

Sales Roles	
Hunter	Develops leads and new business opportunities
Farmer	Aggressively develops and resells existing opportunities
Individual	Is solely responsible for account development and maintenance
Team-based	Works closely with others internally on the account
External	Spends a lot of time at client sites
Internal	Works almost exclusively from the office, via phone, etc.
Short Cycle	Quick or repetitive sales, usually under 2 months start to finish
Long Cycle	Strategic sales, understanding customer's business, 4+ months
Sell End	Sells directly to the end user
Sell Reps	Motivates other representatives to sell products
Simple Sales	Commodity sales, price sensitive, off-the-shelf
Complex Sales	Sells solutions involving multiple components and customization

2. Defining the Most Critical Skills

The second part of the planning stage involves defining a short list of desired skills, based on those relevant roles. Obviously, although Drive is critical, other skills are also important, depending on the position.* The following chart features 17 skills that our research shows are most associated with sales success. The five core skills are those that our research shows are essential to most sales positions: Drive, confidence, persuasion, organization, and relationship skills. We recommend that sales managers assess candidates for each of these skills. Specialized skills, such as analytical, conceptual, and strategic skills, may be

*For simplicity and uniformity, we will use the word "skill" to refer to all competencies relevant to sales positions.

essential in a narrower range of positions. We recommend selecting a total of three to five specialized skills. This keeps the interview process focused and efficient.

CORE SKILLS – Essential in all sales positions
Drive—needs to achieve; loves to compete and win; optimistic and thus certain of victory
Confidence—unfazed by rejection; will persist despite setbacks; inner strength
Persuasion—articulate; builds a good case, taking customer needs into account; closes compellingly
Relationship—easily establishes and maintains relationships with prospects and customers; service-oriented
Organization—disciplined; tracks opportunities and contacts; follows up; juggles multiple tasks; conscientious

SPECIALIZED SKILLS – Unique to your position
Problem Solving—proactively, sometimes creatively, seeks solutions; solves customers' dilemmas
Profit Priority—understands business priorities, sells profitable business
Independent—self-starter, works well without external structure or supervision
Listening—patient; tunes in; will probe and clarify to get a real sense of customers' needs
Tact—considerate; diplomatic; treats others with respect, even if opinions differ
Detail—patient/detailed/timely with necessary product knowledge, reporting, paperwork
Analytical—can dig into needs/problems effectively; adept with numbers
Conceptual—abstract thinker; grasps complexity of customers' situations; develops complex solutions
Strategic—sees big picture and long-range implications; understands customers' strategies
Technical—understands customers' industry, products, and technology
Executive Presence   earns respect in the executive suite; appropriate image
Motivator—(if salesperson is not selling directly to end users) will teach, coach, motivate those who sell product to end user

After completing that discussion with sales management, we now have a detailed specification, or *spec,* of the sales position. The appendix includes a Drive Assessment Planning Form, allowing you to summarize this information for each position.

Next, we interview A players (people who are already doing the job well) at the company. We ask them to elaborate on each skill in the job spec. Their input allows us to refine the spec even further, so we know what each skill looks like on the front line. We also sometimes go on sales calls in order to see for ourselves what it takes for salespeople and their customers to connect in this context.

Some positions, for example, require higher persuasion skills, while others may call for more subtle relationship building. Whatever the case, our ultimate interview will be tailored to identify the best match, given the requirements of the specific sales position.

Step 2

Step 2 of the planning process involves preparing for the interview itself. *It is absolutely critical that we, not the interviewee, control the interview and gain the information we need for a valid assessment of the candidate's potential to succeed in this position.* Remember, the candidates' coaches are recommending the opposite (i.e., that *they* control the interview). It takes structure and discipline to keep candidates on point so we can gather the right data and make accurate observations.

We use a two-hour interview with a very tight agenda which incorporates the following itinerary:

Drive Interview Schedule

(5-10 min) Make small talk, warm up, relax, and establish rapport. Accent the positive.

(15 min) Discuss résumé and career history. Ask candidate for reasons he or she accepted and left each previous job.

(90 min) Ask experience and aptitude questions. Questions are related to what is required to succeed in this position.

Note: Include a halftime break (10 min) midway through the interview.

Probing the Past

Probing the Past is the second *P* in our 3 Ps interview process. *The best way to predict a person's future behavior is to carefully examine what he or she did in the past.* It is therefore critically important that throughout the interview we use *experience questions,* which speak to *behavior,* as opposed to *philosophy questions,* which speak to *aspirations.* Remember, the ultimate name of the game for us is not finding people who *can* (or think they can) sell, it's finding people who *will* sell.

Here is an experience question we like to use in determining Drive: "Tell me about a time when you thought you had a sale but were surprised and disappointed by the prospect or customer. What was your next move?"

Notice we didn't ask, "How did you feel?" It's too easy to give a glib answer to that question. We want to know how the candidate *reacted*. Did this person bounce back quickly? Did he or she learn a lesson and apply it to the next case?

The foregoing example is the kind of question that probes the past for clues that the candidate has applied Driven characteristics before and will do so again for *you*. We will provide a list of such questions later in this chapter.

Patterns

Patterns hold the third *P* key to a successful interview. We structure our process to connect individual questions into a web of patterns which, once identified, are virtually sure to reemerge (both positively and negatively) when the candidate comes to work for you.

Let's say that we want to understand if the candidate can successfully multitask because the position in question requires a variety of actions. We might ask, "Are you better at juggling a number of priorities or projects simultaneously or attacking a few projects one at a time?" A smart candidate, having researched the position, might answer the basic question by stating, "I prefer doing several things at once; it keeps me stimulated."

So far so good, but later in the interview, we loop back and ask when the candidate's confidence is lowest, "When is your confidence the lowest?" If the candidate replies, "When I am overwhelmed with information," whoa! Time out! We need to probe deeper with a follow-up inquiry such as, "Tell me about the last time you got overwhelmed." If the answer includes having "too much on my plate" at the time, we now have contradictory information that requires another follow-up. So, we say, "Give me one more example of a time you were overwhelmed." If the candidate responds with yet another example of having a lot on his or her plate, we have made an important discovery. Now a pattern of breaking down when asked to multitask emerges, despite this candidate's *coached* answer about loving variety.

Establishing patterns is a very enjoyable part of interviewing. It is like detective work: searching for evidence that the candidate is *truly* Driven by uncovering paths he or she has taken in the past—and will no doubt take again in the future—in trying to succeed as a salesperson.

Questions We Love to Ask

We are looking for Driven salespeople. We know that Driven salespeople share three outstanding characteristics: need for achievement; competitiveness; and optimism.

Our two-hour Drive Interview features more than 40 questions, along with related probes, and a final recommendation by a PhD in psychology. We assess each of the skills identified in the job spec. We cannot possibly cover all the questions and their best answers here. But we *can* pass along some of our favorites, which you can use to elevate your own interviewing skills. These questions should give you a feeling for the way psychologists probe for Drive.

Individual Characteristics

Need for Achievement	Look for
1. What kinds of sacrifices have you had to make to be successful?	1. Substantial past sacrifices for success at work (time, other pursuits, etc)
2. Tell me about a few times where you exceeded expectations or went beyond the call of duty.	2. Has regularly exceeded expectations for projects, making sales numbers, customer service
3. How do you know when you've truly succeeded?	3. Has been a sharp critic of own efforts; is tough on self in judging accomplishments
4. Over the last few years, how many hours have you worked in an average week?	4. Has regularly shown effort beyond the typical 40-hour workweek
5. What's the toughest goal you've ever set for yourself? How do you plan to top it?	5. Has accomplished a very challenging work goal; has a specific plan to top that goal
6. Tell me about your last success at work.	6. Tells a story about a major accomplishment and hard work to achieve it
7. What is the hardest you have ever worked to succeed in your job? How often do situations call for that kind of effort? How did you feel about having to work that hard?	7. Has a story about exerting a tremendous effort leading to a major accomplishment; has done so regularly; feels that such effort is simply par for the course
Competitiveness	**Look for**
1. When was the last time you were competitive? Another time?	1. Has more than one recent example (work, home, sports)
2. Where do you rank in the sales team? May I have your permission to contact your boss to ask about your rank?	2. Consistently ranks at or near the top of the sales team and gives permission to verify
3. What is the most fun you have ever had winning a customer over?	3. Tells about enjoying the process of winning over a difficult customer

4. How would your manager rank your competitiveness compared to your peers? What makes your manager see you as competitive?	4. Manager ranks candidate as among most competitive
5. Tell me about the most competitive situation you have ever been in at work. How unusual was it for you?	5. Tells about a competition with coworkers or with competitors over a customer; describes it as a common occurrence
Optimism	**Look for**
1. Describe a sale where your persistence really paid off. Another time?	1. A history of substantial effort to secure a new customer
2. Think back to the last time you lost a deal. What did you do to recover?	2. Quickly put the situation in perspective and bounced back by working on another sale
3. Tell me about a sale that went wrong. What did you attribute it to?	3. Attributes a problem to a temporary, unusual situation out of own control
4. Tell me about the worst customer problem you ever faced. How did you recover?	4. Again, quickly put the situation in perspective and got going on another sale; came back strong after tough times

Combined Characteristics

All Three Characteristics	**Look for**
1. Which parts of your job excite you? Which parts bore you?	1. Enjoys elements of the job involving achievement or competitiveness or resiliency; is rarely or never bored, unless unable to show Drive
2. What do you feel driven to prove?	2. Motivated to prove excellence; wants to be the best; or can rebound from any setback
3. Which of your accomplishments are you most proud of? What about it makes you proud?	3. Takes pride in hard work, surpassing others, or remaining persistent

Here are some examples of probing questions for the other core and specialized skills.

CORE SKILLS
Confidence—Tell me about a time someone rejected you. What did you do?
Persuasion—Give me three examples of closing a difficult sale. What did you say?
Relationship—What have you done in the past 30 days to deepen relationships with key accounts?
Organization—When was the last time you felt overloaded, and how did you recover?

SPECIALIZED SKILLS
Problem Solving—Tell me about a difficult customer dilemma that you resolved.
Profit Priority—Tell me how you balanced volume and profit in your last position.
Independent—Tell me about a time when you took action without explicit permission.
Listening—Tell me about a time when you were with a customer and had to read between the lines to figure out what was important to that customer.
Tact—Tell me about a time when you had to deal with an obnoxious person in an argument.
Detail—Give me a detailed description of how you manage your paperwork and reporting to the company.
Analytical—Have you ever had to make a sale based on analysis of data? Describe the process in detail.
Conceptual—Are you more comfortable dealing with concrete, tangible, black-and-white issues or more abstract, complex concepts?
Strategic—Tell me about a time when you had to adapt to a complex customer strategy.
Technical—What technical aspects of the business do you need to learn to increase your sales?.
Executive Presence—How has your style of interacting with senior executives changed over the years?
Motivator—When did you last have to motivate a rep? How did you do it?

Scoring

Once we have the data to assess Drive and the other skills in the job spec, we are ready to score the candidate. Scoring a candidate's Drive involves two steps.

First, we score the candidate on each of the three key Drive characteristics (need for achievement; competitiveness; and optimism). We use the following scale to summarize our findings:

Rating	Definition
1	Poor
2	Weak
3	Average
4	Good
5	Excellent

Next, we assign a final Drive score using the following system.

Rating	Definition
Green	○ All three elements are rated 4 or 5. ○ This candidate is Driven
Yellow	○ Need for achievement and competitiveness are *both* rated 4 or 5; optimism is 3 ○ This candidate can be developed—with significant effort.
Red	○ One or more of the three Drive elements is rated 1 or 2. ○ This candidate has one or more traits that may compromise performance as a salesperson.

Remember to also rate all other traits in the job spec. Use the 1 through 5 rating system to assign an initial score to each trait (e.g., confidence, persuasiveness, etc.). We use the following table to assign final ratings:

Rating	Definition
Green	Trait is rated 4 or 5. The candidate is clearly skilled in this area.
Yellow	Trait is rated 3. The candidate would benefit by developing this trait.
Red	Trait is rated 1 or 2. The candidate's lack of this trait presents a risk to performance.

Six months after a candidate is hired, we recommend comparing your ratings with their actual performance in each skill. Learning from your mistakes will help you improve as an interviewer.

Following is a SalesDrive assessment report for a candidate who has the Drive to succeed in the position but who has areas in need of improvement to reach his highest potential.

Assessment and Recommendations

Mr. George Seller
Candidate – Sales Representative
United Techmatic
April 9, 2004

SUMMARY AND IMPLICATIONS

Position Requirements – The position of sales representative at United Techmatic requires maintenance of current accounts, finding and securing line extension opportunities, and strengthening customer relationships. The skills critical to success include drive, organization, problem solving, technical knowledge, and relationship skills.

Summary – Mr. George Seller is an experienced salesperson with a results-oriented style. He has numerous skills essential for success as a sales rep for United Techmatic. George is highly driven, with an intense achievement orientation and competitiveness. These traits would contribute to effectiveness in securing line extensions. He is also optimistic, certain of his success and resilient in the face of setbacks. George is organized, able to manage multiple tasks and responsibilities through careful planning. He shows appropriate attention to detail without becoming bogged down in excessive analysis. George has had exposure to plant operations in former positions. He will resolve customer problems efficiently, quickly finding solutions to resolve their concerns. He is willing to go out of his way to help a customer, ensuring satisfaction with his services. Concerning persuasive skills, George closes sales effectively by showing appropriate assertiveness. He is able to listen carefully to uncover unspoken customer needs. George's technical skills are appropriate, including a strong understanding of plant management and knowledge of metallurgy.

George has a strong understanding of business concepts involved in plant management. His intense desire to win and organizational skills allow him to function effectively without direct supervision. George's intellectual ability is appropriate for the position.

Regarding developmental needs, George's intense, impatient style will create difficulty in building relationships with customers who prefer a low-key, informal style. George is also thin-skinned and will occasionally take negative comments personally. Additionally, a difficult or irate customer may cause him to become visibly hurt or frustrated. He will have trouble responding diplomatically when criticized. George's analytical skills and curiosity are average.

Conclusion – In conclusion, Mr. George Seller is a driven and organized candidate with numerous skills essential for success as a sales representative. Based on his performance in the sales assessment, George is recommended for the position with reservations. Our reservations pertain most strongly to his need to develop a thicker skin for dealing with criticism or negative feedback. See pages 2–3 for development recommendations.

CANDIDATE RECOMMENDATION		Chance of Success
RECOMMEND	Good job match. Minimal development needed.	>90%
RECOMMEND (RESERVATIONS)	Good job match. Some development needed.	>80%
NOT RECOMMEND	Skill mismatch, or high risk of performance problems.	<80%

Motivating and Managing Mr. Seller

○ As noted above, George is highly achievement-oriented and will want to work hard to earn his manager's praise. Set goals for him that are challenging but feasible. Recognize his success publicly when he succeeds.

○ Encourage George's efforts to bond with customers. He tends to see lunch or dinner meetings as too casual to be productive. Set a goal of entertaining 10 prospects in his first six months. Give him a mentor skilled at relationship development to get him started.

○ Until he develops more confidence, be aware of George's tendency to take criticism personally. Make sure to balance criticism with recognition of his achievements.

SKILL SUMMARY AND DEVELOPMENT RECOMMENDATIONS				
Skills		**What Needs Development**	**Develop ability**	**Recommendations**
Core Skills				
Drive Needs to achieve; loves to compete and win; certain of success	G		Nil	
Confidence Unfazed by rejection; will persist despite setbacks; inner strength	Y	Can be thin-skinned at times, especially when criticized	Low	1. Sales manager sets stretch-goals and coaches the salesperson through his fears. 2. Salesperson attends the *Basic* and *Interpersonal Intensive* seminars offered by Life Success.
Persuasion Articulate; builds a good case, taking customer needs into account; closes compellingly	G		Med	
Relationship Easily establishes and maintains relationships with prospects and customers	Y	Forceful personality will frustrate some customers	Med	1. Sales manager coaches the salesperson on relationship-building techniques. 2. Salesperson seeks advice from three world-class schmoozers. 3. Salesperson attends the *Basic* and *Interpersonal Intensive* seminars offered by Life Success. 5. Salesperson receives 360° feedback, i.e., information gathered from colleagues, bosses, self, and customers.
Organization Disciplined; tracks opportunities and contacts; follows up; juggles multiple tasks	G		Med	
Specialized Skills				
Problem Solving Proactively, sometimes creatively, seeks solutions; solves customer dilemmas	G		Low	
Independent Self-starter, works well without external structure or supervision	G		Low	
Listening Patient, tunes in, will probe and clarify to get a real sense of customer needs	G		Med	

Specialized Skills				
Tact Considerate; diplomatic; treats others with respect, even if opinions differ	Y	Becomes frustrated when he receives criticism	Med	
Detail Patient/detailed/timely with necessary product knowledge, reporting, paperwork	G		Low	
Analytical Probes needs/problems thoroughly; adept with numbers	Y	Average problem analysis skills and curiosity	Low	1. Sales manager helps the salesperson set up spreadsheets to assure speed and accuracy with calculations. 2. Salesperson is required to rewrite inadequate customer proposals. 3. Salesperson receives 360° feedback.
Conceptual Abstract thinker; grasps complexity of customer situation; develops complex solutions	Y	Favors a concrete approach to understanding problems	Nil	
Technical Understands customer's industry, products, and technology	G		High	

Note: This report is based on a subset of skills identified as critical for this position. There are a total of 17 possible skills available for customization.

G = Green   **Y = Yellow**   **R = Red**

We recommend accepting only candidates scoring green in the Drive category for most sales positions, especially those requiring substantial account acquisition. But you must balance your ratings of Drive with your evaluations of the other key skills for the job. Only *you* can set the bar and arrive at a final decision. However, using this type of assessment to help you identify Drive will give you a strong advantage in making sure that your salespeople have "the right stuff" to begin with.

Summary

◆ The 3 Ps are the key to an effective inter-view:

1. *Planning.* Make sure you do a thorough job spec, using the process outlined in this chapter and the appendix; also make sure to plan your interview from top to bottom.

2. *Probing the Past.* Dig into the candi-date's previous experiences, using the techniques we provide.

3. *Patterns.* Look for patterns in the candi-date's responses and behavior for clues to how the person will behave on the job.

◆ Use the questions in this chapter to assess the three elements of Drive.

◆ Use the rating scale provided in this chap-ter to arrive at a final Drive rating.

◆ Make sure you weigh Drive heavily in your final decision, but also consider the other key skills identified during due dili-gence.

Interviewing Secrets

You can run but you can't hide.

—Joe Louis,
World Heavyweight Champion

As prescribed in chapter 8, the science of interviewing for Drive is composed of the structure of the interview and in asking specific questions designed to identify personality traits and patterns. We now come to the art of interviewing—that is, not only knowing what questions to ask but how to ask them.

Disarming the Candidate

The person on the other side of the table is wearing a filter. It is a filter he or she has constructed to seem as desirable as possible. Our job is to penetrate the filter and get to the real person. We can do so by disarming the candidate's defense system with techniques that neutralize the filtering mechanism. The following are some of our favorites.

Digging for Gold

We never make a judgment about an element of Drive until we are absolutely certain of our diagnosis. To achieve certainty, we often need to probe deeper into the candidate's responses to our initial questions. If we fail to probe the candidate's responses, we may miss a great opportunity to gather important information beyond the prepared answers.

For example, suppose we say, "Tell me about the last time you were competitive." The candidate then replies, "Oh, um . . . the other day."

We would not just leave it there and say, "OK, sounds good. Let's move on." Obviously, we would dig in further to find out what the candidate did the other day that was so competitive. The inquiry would continue along the following lines.

> INTERVIEWER: Tell me about the last time you were competitive.
>
> CANDIDATE: Oh, um . . . the other day.
>
> INTERVIEWER: The other day?

CANDIDATE: Yeah. I was at the gym. I noticed the guy on the elliptical machine next to mine going faster than me. So I sped up to beat him.

INTERVIEWER: What happened then?

CANDIDATE: He noticed me speeding up. So he tried going faster and got winded. I won.

This is a great start; but we always bring it back to the world of work.

INTERVIEWER: How does that competitiveness show up at work?

CANDIDATE: When I'm with a customer, I'm always competitive; thinking about what our company's competitors are quoting and doing whatever it takes to beat it.

INTERVIEWER: OK. So, how could someone in the room tell that you were being competitive? What would you be doing?

CANDIDATE: I'm always asking questions about how satisfied the customer is with our competitor and what we can do to surpass them.

Each time the candidate responded, we dug deeper, getting more specifics and learning more. The key thing to remember about probing is that every question we ask is like a ripe, juicy piece of fruit. All we need to do is keep squeezing until we have gotten all the information possible out of the initial question.

The Echo

This is a great technique designed to ask for more information without making the candidate feel defensive. Simply tilt your head slightly to the side and repeat the key words that interest you, using a questioning tone. For example:

> CANDIDATE: I'm competitive all the time.
>
> INTERVIEWER: All the time?
>
> CANDIDATE: Yes. I dominate every meeting I'm in.
>
> INTERVIEWER: Dominate?
>
> CANDIDATE: Yes. I make sure I'm running the show and putting customers in their place.
>
> INTERVIEWER: Putting customers in their place?
>
> CANDIDATE: Yes. You know, making sure they give me the order or else.

Obviously this candidate needs some relationship skills training, but the point here is that by repeating the person's own words, we encourage the candidate to keep talking until enough has been revealed for us to form an opinion.

Follow-ups

These are simple open-ended questions often starting with the key words Who, What, When, Where, Why, and How. Try to avoid closed-ended questions whenever possible, since closed-ended questions invite one-word answers.

Notice the difference in these two examples:

Example 1: Closed-Ended Question

INTERVIEWER: Did you have trouble dealing with difficult customers?

CANDIDATE: Yes.

Example 2: Open-Ended Question

INTERVIEWER: What was challenging about your most difficult customers?

CANDIDATE: They came across as frustrated and short-tempered. That always scares me . . .

Extreme Questions

These are some of our favorite questions. They will take you right to the heart of the matter. Extreme questions include such words as most, least, biggest, smallest, best, and worst. Let's look at two examples, one with a standard question and one with an extreme question.

Example 1: Standard Question

INTERVIEWER: What was challenging about your last job?

CANDIDATE:	Getting everyone on my team to work together and pulling off some tough assignments.

Example 2: Extreme Question

INTERVIEWER:	What was the most challenging aspect of your last job?
CANDIDATE:	Dealing with my boss.

To reap the full benefit of the extreme question, a follow-up combining the echo and extreme styles is helpful.

INTERVIEWER:	Dealing with your boss? What was most challenging about that?

Fly on the Wall

This is another powerful technique. You can get great clarification about what a candidate is like to work with by using this tactic.

CANDIDATE:	I guess I got a little miffed when that customer called me a jerk.
INTERVIEWER:	Miffed? If I were a fly on the wall, how would I know you were miffed?
CANDIDATE:	Well, I grabbed a hammer and chased him down.

Dealing with Evasive Candidates

Have you ever run across one of these?

INTERVIEWER: Bill, tell me about a time when you wish you were more organized.

CANDIDATE: Oh, gee, let's see. Hmm . . . You know, I really can't think of a time.

Later . . .

INTERVIEWER: Bill, tell me about a sale you made that was unprofitable.

CANDIDATE: Hmm. You know, I really can't think of one. They've all been profitable really.

Later . . .

INTERVIEWER: Bill, what kinds of sales are most challenging for you?

CANDIDATE: Oh . . .um . . . none, really. I've never really had trouble selling anything.

Well, Bill, consider this your first time.

We have all experienced evasive candidates. They give quick, one-word answers; provide little elaboration; and can't seem to think of a single mistake they've ever made. Taken at face value, they are perfect specimens of salespeople who simply don't want to waste our time with the details of their many accomplishments.

But we know better. These folks are being evasive for a reason. They often have something to hide, whether it's a bad experience or their lack of experience.

Many new sales managers fall into the trap of unconsciously colluding with the evasive candidate. They allow the candidate to give short answers with little detail. They move on to the next question quickly to avoid the awkward silence. The problem is that once the candidate knows that a quick answer will be accepted, it's the only kind you will get.

Let's discuss a few tactics to deal with evasive candidates. We recommend starting out with a gentler technique. But, if they do not cooperate, confront them about their behavior.

"What about it?" Questions

"What about it?" questions are a great first strategy for cracking a candidate's defenses. For example, when asked about a previous job, a candidate may seem skittish and say, "Yes, that job sure was a tough one," and then look at you as if to imply, "Next question." The candidate may also try to move on to another subject at this point. But there's no way you're going to leave gold like this laying around. You can reply with, "Back to your last job for a minute; what about it was hard?" This follow-up targets the heart of the issue and forces the candidate to give you more information.

The Magic Wand Question

This technique is great when a candidate is reluctant to reveal the details of previous underperformance at work. Simply ask the candidate in a disarming, creative way what would have made the situation better. Such a tactic will typically cause candidates to drop their defenses. Here's an example:

INTERVIEWER: What about the last job was so hard?

CANDIDATE: The environment was really tough to work in.

INTERVIEWER: OK, if we had a magic wand and could improve three things about that job so you would never want to leave, what would they be?

CANDIDATE: The boss would be less demanding; my assistant would not have quit; and my coworkers would be more intelligent.

Avoiding "Why" Questions

Here's another tip for getting past a candidate's defenses. If you are interviewing someone who is having trouble disclosing information without looking nervous, avoid "Why" questions. In an interview setting, the word "why" can have a slightly accusing tone, especially to someone who is scared about revealing something personal. "Why" tends to make evasive people more evasive. Instead, rephrase these inquiries into "What" or "How" questions. For example, instead of asking, "Why did you do that?" try

"What caused you to make that decision?" This is a subtle point, but it can be extraordinarily useful in helping a nervous candidate relax enough to open up and tell you something.

Confrontation

So, you've tried to play nice but the candidate is still shutting you out, eh? Well, here's Plan B for handling evasive candidates: confront them.

Every now and then, you will get a candidate who gives nothing but terse, one- or two-word answers. Here's an example:

> INTERVIEWER: Tell me about a time when you went out of your way to help a customer out.

> CANDIDATE: Yeah, you know, that happens a lot.

> INTERVIEWER: OK. Can you give me a specific example?

> CANDIDATE: Sure, you know, just the other day, I helped a customer.

> INTERVIEWER: OK. What happened? Can you give me the details?

> CANDIDATE: I can't remember the details exactly. Someone just needed some help, and I was there. Happens all the time.

We usually let something like this slide one or two times because we have so many questions to get through. However, when the candidate keeps the evasive wall up past that point, we call him or her on it.

For example:

INTERVIEWER: I get the impression that some of these questions are tough for you to answer.

[Silence]

CANDIDATE: Yeah. It's just hard to come up with specifics.

INTERVIEWER: Yes. I understand. I know it's a lot to remember. But rest assured, you have plenty of time to think. It's very important for me to get these details so we can determine if this is the kind of job you are looking for. Also, I will need to know what kinds of specific details to ask your references about. As we go on, just let me know if you need some extra time, and I will wait as long as you need. Let's try a different question.

Move on to your next question. Later, circle back to the initially evaded question. If the candidate is still evasive, this person likely is trying to hide something. Proceed with extreme caution.

Red Flags

As you proceed with the interview, you will likely be assessing several skills in addition to Drive, such as organization, relationship skills, and persuasiveness. Please note that there are a few candidate traits that indicate that the person may have tendencies that will cause performance problems on the job. These red flags are often evident but go undetected during the selection process. Industrial psychologists Neil Witmer and Jeff Grip in a 2002 report identified several of these behavior patterns. The table that follows summarizes the most problematic behaviors. Take it with you to your interviews and look it over once before you begin and once at halftime. Make sure that you look closely when any of these traits seems evident.

Evidence of any of these behaviors during interviews should be probed thoroughly. However, these red flags are not foolproof indicators of poor performance. In a given job, one may be a fatal flaw while others are tolerated. A good rule of thumb is that one of these red flags indicates caution, and two or more indicate risk, raising serious doubt as to a successful job match.

Table 1: Red Flags Checklist

Limited Intelligence	○ black-and-white thinking—limited depth ○ has difficulty discussing abstract ideas (low conceptual skills)
Extreme Intelligence	○ thinks too quickly—hard to follow—shoots over others' heads ○ bores too quickly ○ fails to filter input—makes things too complex—unable to give simple answers
Lack of Focus	○ distracted on tangents during interview ○ undisciplined work habits—inconsistent follow-through

Highly Controlling	○ compulsion to be in charge of everything—protects own position and turf ○ poor listening skills—interrupts—dominates interviews and conversations ○ frustrates with schedule changes
Excessive Perfectionism and Rigidity	○ stiff personality ○ uncomfortable with ambiguous questions ○ intolerant of others' ideas and operating styles ○ has trouble accepting "healthy mistakes"
Arrogance and Condescension	○ "better-than-thou" or "smarter-than-thou" ○ prone to vulgarity ○ has difficulty admitting shortcomings ○ overly attracted to power, prestige, and perks
Overly Analytical and Linear	○ speaks in an overly linear and calculating manner ○ requires excessive data—risk-averse ○ hesitates to demand "out-of-the-box" results when required ○ needs a lot of structure (conversations, directions, assignments)
Overly Polished and Guarded	○ hung up on dress and appearance ○ postures an overly positive view of self and past performance ○ apprehensive to discuss personal shortcomings
Lack of Confidence	○ intimidated by higher-ups or strong personalities ○ self-conscious in interviews—overly apologetic—needs approval—avoids conflict ○ avoids social involvement—prefers being a loner
Self-Absorbed	○ more focused on own performance than getting results through others ○ uncomfortable in social situations—lacks skill in persuasion and alliances ○ shows more evidence of "taking" than "giving"
Emotionally Uncontrolled	○ prone to outbursts or inappropriate intensity ○ easily frustrated by obstacles ○ fails to tune into impact on others
Excessive Job Moves	○ restless—bored—hyperactive ○ shows bad judgment by having chosen bad companies or bad bosses ○ position downsized/eliminated multiple times

Source: Witmer and Grip 2002. Used with permission.

Summary

◆ Getting past a candidate's defenses requires several advanced interviewing skills.

◆ Never make a judgment about an element of Drive unless you are absolutely certain. Keep probing to uncover the details in candidate responses. Several techniques are helpful for doing so:

— *Digging for Gold*. Keep asking for greater detail until you have the whole story; steer general character information into a work context.

— *The Echo*. Repeat with a questioning tone the key words the candidate has said.

— *Follow-ups*. Ask open-ended questions starting with *Who, What, When, Where, Why*, or *How*. Avoid closed-ended questions, which require only a yes or no answer.

— *Extreme Questions*. Ask questions including such words as most, least, best, or worst to get to the heart of the matter.

— *Fly on the Wall*. To get specifics about a situation, ask the candidate, "If I were a fly on the wall, what would I have seen you doing?

◆ There are several great ways to handle evasive candidates:

— *"What about it?" Questions*. Ask what about the situation in question was particularly difficult.

— *The Magic Wand Question*. Ask what three things the candidate would change about a difficult situation if we had a magic wand.

— *Avoiding "Why?" Questions*. "Why" can sound accusatory to a nervous candidate. Rephrase *Why* questions into *What* or *How* questions.

— *Confrontation*. Occasionally you need to firmly, but gently, let an obstinately evasive candidate know that he or she must provide you with more information on a question so you can make a hiring decision.

◆ Look closely for *red flags* in the candidate's behavior that may compromise performance. They include arrogance, being overly guarded, and lack of emotional control.

Part Three:

Developing Your Current Salespeople

10
Chapter

Assessing and Enhancing Your Current Team

To select the wrong person for a job is a common mistake; not to remove him or her is a fatal weakness.

—Anonymous

We have discussed how to identify and hire *candidates* with Drive and the other key skills necessary to succeed in your sales positions. But what about your current salespeople? Many of the same principles apply, but the increased complexity of the situation requires careful consideration.

Most business owners or sales managers already know whether they have strong, mediocre, or poor performers. The quarterly numbers tell the story. But only the most advanced sales managers *truly* understand whether their salespeople can be developed to sell *more* or have reached their limits. These successful sales managers assess their sales team's *potential* as well as its performance.

Understanding each salesperson's potential allows managers to make the necessary staffing decisions to substantially increase sales. Managers can then conduct targeted training where the investments will really pay off, versus wasting money on training underperformers who cannot improve. Luckily, underperforming salespeople often can be redeployed to inside or support positions where they can be more productive; but they should systematically be assessed and, if necessary, replaced by hiring A players for the frontline sales positions that make or break the company.

In this chapter we will explain how top sales managers assess their current team's potential. We will also show you how to apply the SalesDrive process to your current team to identify the richest opportunities for development.

A, B, and C Players

As a first step, we need to realistically determine what our current team looks like. We need to find out how much of a problem we really have with underperformers. This step is essential for letting us know which of our salespeople will benefit from the Drive Interview. Before we begin, let's review a few terms.

A Players are salespeople who are performing above our expectations in their positions. They are exceeding budget and doing an exemplary job of fulfilling their responsibilities, whether in account acquisition or maintenance. Customers love them.

B Players are salespeople who are meeting our expectations but would benefit from development. They may have the basic skills for the job, including Drive, but may still be new to the position, or they may have a few skills deficits that are amenable to development. For example, they may need to develop their listening or organizational skills.

C Players, as discussed in chapter 5, are salespeople who consistently fail to meet your expectations. Their numbers are significantly below goal. They lack *several* basic sales skills, such as relationship building, organization, or confidence. They frustrate customers. We likely would not hire them again. If these people are also low on Drive, they have little to no development potential.

In chapter 5, you determined how many C players you are carrying as well as the cost of waiting to deal with them. *Note:* If you have skipped that step, go back to chapter 5 and do it now. It is critical for a responsible sales manager to understand how much the company is losing in annual revenues due to C players.

C players who *lack* Drive are almost impossible to change. The personality traits that are holding them back from selling were solidified by the time they were young adults. It would require a lot of money and expensive therapy to improve their performance even marginally. B players, however, often have Drive and can be developed to sell *more*.

> **Most companies find that targeting B players is the most efficient use of their assessment efforts.**

Assessing and culling your team to include only A and B players sounds like a no-brainer, right? After all, what could possibly keep an intelligent sales manager from making sure the existing team has nothing but potential producers? Unfortunately, four misconceptions get in the way of assessing current talent. Each of these roadblocks robs companies of millions of dollars in lost revenue and training costs. We call these classic errors the Four Fallacies. Let's review them now.

The Four Fallacies

1. I Know My People Well Enough

We have heard dozens of sales managers say, "I know my people well enough." Indeed, you may have known many of these people for years. Some may clearly be Drivers. Others may obviously be underperformers. But what about the salespeople in the middle of the road? A few may perform adequately. But for how long? Do you know for sure that they are Driven? Will they improve next quarter or crap out? What will it cost you if they fail? Even if your salespeople are paid totally on commission, what opportunities for new business will you lose? The *only way* to answer this question is by putting those salespeople through the Drive assessment process and *defining* rather than *guessing* about their potential.

2. Salespeople Are Expendable

It's a sad fact that many organizations see salespeople as an expendable resource. Salespeople, the very lifeblood of the organization, are looked on as disposable, able to be quickly replaced. Those who hold this view simply churn salespeople, hiring warm bodies. They often don't take the time to assess *potential* A players right underneath their noses. These sales managers are reluctant to spend the time and money necessary to identify salespeople with high potential.

Consequently, their high-potential B players get frustrated and leave to become A players elsewhere. Then the "churn 'em and burn 'em" company wastes more money hiring new warm bodies.

For the most part, successful business owners and CEOs who invest in their sales teams' development reap the rewards of stronger sales. Like good sports coaches, they maximize their use of current A and B players; they redeploy or replace the C players. Their reward for these efforts: *a winning team*.

3. This Could Make Me Look Bad

Here's a scary thought: some sales managers avoid formally assessing their sales teams out of *fear*. They are afraid that identifying one or more C players will make them look bad, as recruiters and managers, to their CEO. Some may be afraid that the inadequacies of their hiring policy will be exposed. Others may be deliberately ignoring or hiding a few C players. So, they make excuses to avoid the process. They tell themselves that they are simply too busy, they cannot afford the distraction this quarter, their budget is too low, they have other priorities, and so on.

It is understandable that sales managers who have not been exposed to the Drive model could have *hired* a few underperformers. It is also understandable that extenuating circumstances may have gotten in the way of *upgrading* their current team for a few quarters. But it is *inexcusable* that this avoidance and coddling continue indefinitely.

Contrary to their fears, sales managers who put their foot down and decide to accept nothing short of A and B players make a powerful statement to the CEO. By conducting Drive Interviews with their current salespeople, these managers put a stake in the ground, making it clear that lackluster performance will *not* be tolerated. They earn the CEO's respect for removing underperformers and recruiting stars.

4. I Don't Want to Hurt Anyone's Feelings

Many sales managers have a personal bond with their team. They are close to their people and want to see them succeed. They dread the idea of firing a C player whom they see as a friend. They will continue to give this person "one more chance" because "maybe things will get better next quarter." Although they mean well, such managers are lying to themselves and hurting everyone in the process.

If a salesperson is a chronic underperformer in spite of repeated developmental efforts, this person is unlikely to improve and would likely be much happier in another position that allowed him or her to succeed. Strong sales managers know they need to make tough decisions. Sales managers who ignore the talent level of current salespeople are ignoring *the* major part of their responsibilities to the organization.

Weak sales managers trade results for warm, fuzzy feelings. Most CEOs are not pleased with this trade-off. To put it in perspective, imagine the coach of a losing pro sports team holding a press conference and saying, "We certainly could make some changes here if we wanted to. But, frankly, I don't want to hurt anyone's feelings. So we'll just go out there with what we've got and hope for the best."

Each of these Four Fallacies has the same result: *the status quo is maintained at the expense of the company's performance.* Strong sales managers do not give in to these fallacies. They are *relentless* in their pursuit of excellence. Their teams know this and respect their high standards. The salespeople may share an occasional beer with the manager, but they also know that they will be held accountable for their performance—no excuses.

The SalesDrive Process

Sales managers need to know how to audit their current team's talent. This simple but effective method, called the SalesDrive process, allows companies to answer three key questions:

1. Can your B players be developed to sell more, or have they peaked?

2. How can you motivate high-potential B players to reach the A level?

3. Do any of your C players have the ability to improve, or should they be redeployed?

Here are three steps we advise companies to take in answering these questions when we are asked to participate in the incumbent assessment process.

Step 1: Benchmarking

The first step in the SalesDrive process is very similar to the Planning phase we discussed in chapter 8. We interview sales management to determine the skills essential for the job. We conduct this interview using the Sales Manager Planning Form in the appendix. We also interview top performers to find out the things they do to show these skills. We help sales managers divide their team into A, B, and C players, based on performance. Salespeople are then selected to participate in the Drive assessment.

Step 2: "Skills and Potential" Assessment

Next, a Drive assessment professional interviews each salesperson to conclusively determine that person's level of Drive and *all other key skills*. Most important, the Drive assessment professional also determines each person's ability to improve.

Step 3: Management Debriefing

This final step is a critical developmental milestone for a sales organization. We meet with management to discuss each salesperson's results and the team's prognosis for improvement. First, we discuss the results of the assessment in conjunction with each salesperson's previous performance. We discuss strategies for motivating and mentoring each person, based on his or her unique psychological characteristics. For example, we may recommend a stern, blunt approach for one salesperson but a more gentle, indirect style for another. *For each salesperson who is capable of development, management receives specific steps for getting him or her to the next level.*

High-Potential B Players

As we stated earlier, some B players are capable of improvement. They have the potential to become As. Let's take a closer look at this group, since it represents the best chance for true growth.

High-potential B players have the psychological foundation to succeed in sales. They are Driven, and they have a thick skin and solid social skills. But they also have one or two rough edges that occasionally hold them back. They may need to learn more advanced relationship skills for bonding with customers; they may need to brush up on their listening skills or advanced persuasion techniques. Conversely, they may have strong levels of all essential traits but simply need to build industry experience.

Whatever their needs are, these B-level Drivers need focused guidance to improve. Show them what skills or knowledge they need to build, and they will work hard to make it happen. If the training budget is limited, this is the group that will provide the biggest bang for the buck. These people will soak up the information and look for ways to apply it in the field.

Additionally, the Drive assessment tells us how to manage and motivate producers, given their unique psychological characteristics. For example, a Driven B player may habitually disregard the need to bond and schmooze with customers. He or she may be too business-focused in customer meetings. A psychological interview might show that deep down, this B player fears appearing frivolous and avoids small talk. When the salesperson recognizes this fear, it becomes possible to change his or her view of small talk and work on techniques to bond more closely with customers. The Drive assessment will identify the best training resources to build this skill.

The following is a SalesDrive assessment report for an incumbent B player who has potential to improve.

Assessment and Recommendations

Ms. Jane Driver
Regional Sales Manager
Acme Manufacturing
February 12, 2005

SUMMARY AND IMPLICATIONS

Position Requirements – The position of Regional Sales Manager at Acme Manufacturing requires identification and opening of new accounts as well as expansion of established accounts. The essential sales skills for the position include drive, confidence, persuasion, and relationship skills.

Summary – Ms. Jane Driver is an ambitious, disciplined regional sales manager with numerous traits essential for the role. Jane shows the drive necessary for success in any sales position. She has the ambition, competitiveness, and optimism necessary for dealing proactively and resiliently with the challenges inherent in sales. She will work hard, taking on extra responsibilities to exceed her manager's expectations. Jane's drive will also compel her to develop her skills. She is independent and able to work effectively without direct supervision. Jane understands when to take the initiative and when to ask for help. In dealing with prospects or current customers, Jane takes a low-pressure, highly service-oriented approach. She enjoys developing creative solutions to customer problems. Jane is highly organized and will use a focused, disciplined approach to account maintenance and follow-up.

Concerning developmental needs, Jane has a few traits that will reduce her effectiveness as a regional sales manager. Most important, regarding listening skills, Jane needs to improve her ability to focus on her audience without getting distracted by her own ideas. Her mind moves quickly, and she can become excessively talkative when she finds a topic personally interesting. Jane also occasionally interrupts when she gets excited about a topic. These difficulties with listening will frustrate an impatient customer. Jane can also get a bit defensive if she feels her expertise is being questioned. At such times, she can come across as condescending or a know-it-all. Regarding relationship skills, Jane's difficulties with listening will occasionally hold her back from making the customer feel understood. Additionally, Jane needs to make sure that her priorities are in alignment with her manager's goals. Although Jane will focus on the most profitable potential accounts, she is still learning prospecting strategies appropriate for the industry.

Regarding Jane's approach to problem solving, she likes to reduce ambiguity and tries to develop systems if possible. She will spend substantial time analyzing an unfamiliar issue. However, Jane can run into trouble with more routine issues. If she is familiar with an area, she can become overly impulsive, acting without gathering enough information. This is a side effect of her drive, but it can get her into trouble if she encounters a seemingly familiar problem with a twist.

Conclusion – In summary, Ms. Jane Driver is an ambitious regional sales manager with several skills important for success in the position. She will take her performance up a notch by focusing on her ability to listen carefully to customers. By doing so, Jane will also improve her persuasiveness and relationship skills. Jane's ambition and strong work ethic will compel her to work hard at improving her skills and increasing her versatility.

Motivating and Managing Ms. Driver

○ Jane is a bright and ambitious thinker who occasionally will have trouble staying on the task at hand. As Jane begins in the position, provide her with guidance on whether her efforts support or distract from her manager's goals.

○ Allow Jane to exercise her creative side by assigning her some projects requiring creative thinking that she can own and enjoy. Recognize her accomplishments when she succeeds in these tasks.

○ Jane needs to develop her ability to listen carefully to her audience. The listening skills courses outlined below would be beneficial.

○ Jane needs to address her tendency to come across as condescending at times. The Basic and Interpersonal Intensive seminars offered by Life Success would be effective in addressing this issue.

SKILL SUMMARY AND DEVELOPMENT RECOMMENDATIONS				
Skills		What Needs Development	Develop ability	Recommendations
Core Skills				
Drive Needs to achieve; loves to compete and win; certain of success	G		Nil	
Confidence Unfazed by rejection; will persist despite setbacks; inner strength	Y	Can come across as condescending if her expertise is questioned	Low	1. Sales manager sets stretch-goals and coaches the salesperson through her fears. 2. Salesperson attends the *Basic* and *Interpersonal Intensive* seminars offered by Life Success.
Persuasion Articulate; builds a good case, taking customer needs into account; closes compellingly	Y	Difficulties with listening will reduce her ability to persuade prospects or current customers	Med	1. Salesperson receives 360° feedback, i.e., information gathered from colleagues, bosses, self, and customers. 2. Salesperson reads *Let's Get Real or Let's Not Play,* by Mahan Khalsa. 3. Salesperson reads *The Psychology of Persuasion* by Kevin Hogan.
Relationship Easily establishes and maintains relationships with prospects and customers	Y	Listening difficulties will reduce her ability to make the customer understood, or to bond closely	Med	1. Sales manager coaches the salesperson on relationship-building techniques. 2. Salesperson seeks advice from three world-class schmoozers. 3. Salesperson reads *Mr. Shmooze* by Richard Abraham. 4. Salesperson attends the *Basic* and *Interpersonal Intensive* seminars offered by Life Success. 5. Salesperson receives 360° feedback.
Organization Disciplined; tracks opportunities and contacts; follows up; juggles multiple tasks	G		Med	
Specialized Skills				
Problem Solving Proactively, sometimes creatively, seeks solutions; solves customer dilemmas	Y	Can become overly impulsive and attempt to solve a problem without gathering enough information	Low	1. Salesperson solicits ideas from a colleague or mentor who is highly creative and skilled at solving customer problems. 2. Salesperson forms a task team, with customer representation, to tackle seemingly unsolvable problems. 3. Salesperson reads *Let's Get Real or Let's Not Play*, by Mahan Khalsa. 4. Salesperson receives 360° feedback.

Specialized Skills				
Profit Priority Understands business priorities, sells profitable business	**Y**	Still learning prospecting strategies appropriate for the industry	Med	1. Sales manager clearly defines sales objectives and quarterly performance measures. 2. Sales manager conducts weekly priority reviews. 3. Sales manager or finance manager coaches the salesperson to understand profit contribution formulas. 4. Sales manager provides candid feedback on salesperson's habits and agendas that are not in alignment with business priorities.
Independent Self-starter, works well without external structure or supervision	**G**		Low	
Listening Patient, tunes in, will probe and clarify to get a real sense of customer needs	**R**	Becomes excessively talkative and interrupts when she gets excited or finds a topic interesting	Med	1. Salesperson reads *Listening: The Forgotten Skill* by Madelyn Burley-Allen 2. Salesperson works with HR/training to help teach courses in Active Listening. 3. Salesperson receives 360° feedback.
Motivator Will teach, coach, motivate those who sell product to end user	**Y**	Difficulties with listening will reduce her ability to motivate distributors	Med	1. Sales manager clearly defines expectations and the role of the sales leader. 2. Salesperson receives 360° feedback.

Note: This report is based on a subset of skills identified as critical for this position. There are a total of 17 possible skills available for customization.

G = Green   **Y = Yellow**   **R = Red**

Using a Psychologist to Assess Sales Talent

We designed this book to inform you about and provide basic techniques for identifying Driven salespeople. Its principles and methods can give you a substantial advantage over your uninformed competitors. We are certain that many sales managers and business owners who might not ordinarily seek professional assistance will be helped by this book. However, no book on hiring can truly match the power of a psychologist for conclusively identifying Drive in candidates and current salespeople.

Expertise in Assessing Human Motivation

Psychologists have years of training in the *hidden,* inner motives that make people tick. They know how to quickly spot inconsistencies in a candidate's story. Psychologists can tell when a current employee lacks the desire to improve. They understand how to identify the three elements of Drive and can accurately assess other key skills, including confidence and persuasion.

Industrial psychologists are trained in each step of the interview process we have outlined here. They will research the job thoroughly, using the expertise of your current top performers, to create an accurate job spec. They will test and interview your candidates, adhering to EEOC guidelines. Finally, they will provide an impartial, unbiased opinion on your candidates or current people.

Hiring an Industrial Psychologist

Your choice of industrial psychologist is as important as your sales hiring decisions. The psychologist will likely be making hiring recommendations. Here are a few things to look for in an industrial psychologist.

1. Make sure the psychologist's approach is tailored to your business, not a cookie-cutter plan. The psychologist should adapt his or her process to your company's unique needs.

2. The psychologist should use valid tools and processes. The psychologist should be able to provide evidence of the validity of his or her tests and interview procedures.

3. Most important, the psychologist should have expertise in conducting psychological interviews of *salespeople*. If the psychologist is not experienced in interviewing sales candidates, he or she may contribute little to your ultimate success.

We hope that this chapter has clarified the benefits of using expert assistance to assess sales candidates. A salesperson's performance is crucial to a company's success. Because of the unique psychological challenges of sales, a salesperson's personality determines his or her capability to perform. This is why professional assessment is essential to make sure you invest only in salespeople who will succeed.

Summary

- Top sales managers know each of their direct reports' potential for improvement.

- There are three levels of sales performance:

  1. *A players:* salespeople who regularly surpass your expectations.

  2. *B players:* salespeople who meet your expectations but could use some improvement.

  3. *C players:* salespeople who consistently fail to meet your expectations and are deficient in multiple essential skills.

- It is critical for responsible sales managers to learn how much they are losing in annual revenues due to underperformance by C players.

- Managers should avoid the Four Fallacies that get in the way of upgrading current salespeople:

  1. "I know my people well enough."

  2. "Salespeople are expendable."

  3. "This could make me look bad."

  4. "I don't want to hurt anyone's feelings."

- B players usually represent the richest opportunity for development.

◆ The SalesDrive process addresses three key questions:

1. Can your B players be developed to sell more, or have they peaked?

2. How can you motivate high-potential B players to reach the A level?

3. Do any of your C players have the ability to improve performance, perhaps in support of A or B players?

◆ There are three steps taken in answering these key questions:

1. *Benchmarking.* Sales managers and top performers are interviewed to determine skills essential for the job; current sales team is divided into A, B, and C players.

2. *Drive assessment.* Those selected to participate in Drive assessment are interviewed to determine their development potential and training needs.

3. *Management debriefing.* Interviewer discusses with managers the assessment results and prognosis for improvement for each team member.

◆ Sales managers must take action to reassign or release underperformers who lack potential and replace them with A players.

The Most Important Decisions of Your Career

Plans are only good intentions unless they
immediately degenerate into hard work.

—Peter Drucker

The sales decisions you make as a business owner or manager determine both the success of your company and your quality of life. They are among the most important decisions you will ever make.

This book has provided you with powerful tools to make informed decisions about improving your sales team's performance—*and* your company's bottom line. We have defined Drive and broken it down into its three elements: need for achievement; competitiveness; and optimism. We have seen how each element is essential for creating the *perfect storm* of passion that fuels great athletes and superstar salespeople alike.

We have discussed the enormous costs associated with underperformance in sales. You have determined these costs for your own company. We hope you have come to the conclusion that it is far cheaper to screen in advance for high-potential performers than it is to carry under-performing salespeople and pray they will improve.

We discussed prescreening for Drive. You have learned interviewing techniques for getting a more accurate read on a candidate. You have also learned a process for assessing your *current* salespeople to determine who has the *potential* to improve.

Most important, you now have the answer to a question most sales managers and business owners have puzzled over for decades: *How do I determine if a salesperson has the potential to meet my expectations?*

In our experience as business owners and advisers, the mis-hiring and carrying of low-potential salespeople is often the number one waste of company resources and the biggest single opportunity cost in the company's life cycle. While there are a number of reasons salespeople succeed or fail, it all starts with potential—potential that is hardwired in the form of Drive.

There is nothing easy about demanding that only A and B players work at your company, but that is exactly what the most successful professional sports franchises, the most elite universities, and the most powerful sales organizations do. They do not compromise. While the assessment process requires patience, discipline, and diligence, the rewards can be staggering as you finally elevate your sales team to its highest and best performance: the performance of champions.

Appendix

Drive Assessmant Planning Form

Step 1. Define Sales Roles: For each pair, check the role that applies to the position. If both roles apply, check both.

Sales Roles	
Hunter	Develops leads and new business opportunities
Farmer	Aggressively develops and resells existing opportunities
Individual	Is solely responsible for account development and maintenance
Team-based	Works closely with others internally on the account
External	Spends a lot of time at client sites
Internal	Works almost exclusively from the office, via phone, etc.
Short Cycle	Quick or repetitive sales, usually under 2 months start to finish
Long Cycle	Strategic sales, understanding customer's business, 4+ months
Sell End	Sells directly to the end user
Sell Reps	Motivates other representatives to sell products
Simple Sales	Commodity sales, price sensitive, off-the-shelf
Complex Sales	Sells solutions involving multiple components and customization

Step 2. Review the Core Skills.

CORE SKILLS – Essential in all sales positions
Drive—needs to achieve; loves to compete and win; optimistic and thus certain of victory
Confidence—unfazed by rejection; will persist despite setbacks; inner strength
Persuasion—articulate; builds a good case, taking customer needs into account; closes compellingly
Relationship—easily establishes and maintains relationships with prospects and customers; service-oriented
Organization—disciplined; tracks opportunities and contacts; follows up; juggles multiple tasks; conscientious

Step 3. Select up to 3 Specialized Skills.

SPECIALIZED SKILLS – Unique to your position
Problem Solving—proactively, sometimes creatively, seeks solutions; solves customers' dilemmas
Profit Priority—understands business priorities, sells profitable business
Independent—self-starter, works well without external structure or supervision
Listening—patient; tunes in; will probe and clarify to get a real sense of customers' needs
Tact—considerate; diplomatic; treats others with respect, even if opinions differ
Detail—patient/detailed/timely with necessary product knowledge, reporting, paperwork
Analytical—can dig into needs/problems effectively; adept with numbers
Conceptual—abstract thinker; grasps complexity of customers' situations; develops complex solutions
Strategic—sees big picture and long-range implications; understands customers' strategies
Technical—understands customers' industry, products, and technology
Executive Presence—earns respect in the executive suite; appropriate image
Motivator—(if salesperson is not selling directly to end users) will teach, coach, motivate those who sell product to end user

Notes

Full source citations appear in the Bibliography that follows this list of source notations.

Introduction
> *See*
> Churchill et al. 1985
> FastScripts 2005

Chapter 1   Drive: The Foundation of Success
> *See*
> Brewer 1994
> Vinchur et al. 1998

Chapter 2   The Need to Achieve
> *See*
> Croner 2004
> McClelland 1961
> McClelland et al. 1976
> Soyer, Rovenpor, and Kopelman 1999
> Tucker-Ladd 1997
> *Vinchur et al. 1998*

Chapter 3   The Thrill of Competition
> *See*
> Brewer 1994
> Brown, Cron, and Slocum 1998
> Greenberg, Weinstein, and Sweeney 2001
> Krishnan, Netemeyer, and Boles 2003

Chapter 4   Optimism
See
Schulman 1995, 1999
Seligman and Schulman 1986
Strutton and Lumpkin 1993

Chapter 5   The High Cost of Low Performance
See
Future Foundation and SHL 2004
Ingram, Schwepker, and Hutson 1992

Chapter 6   Testing: The First Step
See
Cortina et al. 2000
Van Iddekinge, Raymark, and Roth 2005

Chapter 7   The Rules of Interview Engagement
See
Barrick, Patton, and Haugland 2000
Huffcutt et al. 2001
Pulakos and Schmitt 1995

Chapter 9   Interviewing Secrets
See
Witmer and Grip 2002

Bibliography

Barling, J., E. K. Kelloway, and D. Cheung. 1996. Time management and achievement striving interact to predict car sales performance. *Journal of Applied Psychology* 81:821–26.

Barrick, M. R., G. K. Patton, and S. N. Haugland. 2000. Accuracy of interviewer judgments of job applicants' personality traits. *Personnel Psychology* 53:925–51.

Bartkus, K. N., M. F. Peterson, and D. N. Bellenger. 1989. Type A behavior, experience, and salesperson performance. *Journal of Personal Selling and Sales Management* 9:11–18.

Bluen, S. D., J. Barling, and W. Burns. 1990. Predicting sales performance, job satisfaction, and depression by using the achievement strivings and impatience-irritability dimensions of Type A behavior. *Journal of Applied Psychology* 75:212–16.

Brewer, G. 1994. Mind reading. *Sales and Marketing Management* 146:82–87.

Brown, B. P., W. L. Cron, and J. W. Slocum Jr. 1998. Effects of trait competitiveness and perceived intraorganizational competition on salesperson goal setting and performance. *Journal of Marketing* 62:88–98.

Chang, J. 2003. Born to sell? *Sales and Marketing Management* 155:34–38.

Churchill, G. A. Jr., N. M. Ford, S. W. Hartley, and O. C. Walker Jr. 1985. The determinants of salesperson performance: A meta-analysis. *Journal of Marketing Research* 22:103–18.

Cortina, J. M., N. B. Goldstein, S. C. Payne, H. K. Davison, and S. W. Gillard. 2000. The incremental validity of interview scores over and above cognitive ability and conscientiousness scores. *Personnel Psychology* 53:325–51.

Croner, C. J. 2004. DriveTest technical report. SalesDrive, Oak Brook, IL.

FastScripts by ASAP Sports. 2005. 87th PGA Championship Baltusrol Golf Club interview transcript Tuesday, August 09, 2005: An interview with Tiger Woods. http://i.pga.com/pga/images/events/2005/pgachamp/ pdf/ interview_080905_twoods.pdf (accessed June 1, 2006).

Future Foundation and SHL. 2004. Getting the edge in the new people economy. www.futurefoundation.net/publications.php?disp=117 (accessed January 11, 2006).

Greenberg, H., H. Weinstein, and P. Sweeney. 2001. *How to Hire and Develop Your Next Top Performer: The Five Qualities That Make Salespeople Great*. New York: McGraw-Hill.

Huffcutt, A. I., J. A. Weekley, W. H. Wiesner, T. G. Degroot, and C. Jones. 2001. Comparison of situational and behavior description interview questions for higher-level positions. *Personnel Psychology* 54:619–44.

Ingram, T. N., C. H. Schwepker Jr., and D. Hutson. 1992. Why salespeople fail. *Industrial Marketing Management* 21:225–30.

Jones, R., and R. Sala. 1996. Do athletes make good reps? *Sales and Marketing Management* 148:92–96.

Krishnan, B. C., R. G. Netemeyer, and J. S. Boles. 2003. Self-efficacy, competitiveness, and effort as antecedents of salesperson performance. *Journal of Personal Selling and Sales Management* 22:285–95.

Lee, C., and D. J. Gillen. 1989. Relationship of Type A behavior pattern, self-efficacy perceptions on sales performance. *Journal of Organizational Behavior* 10:75–81.

Matteson, M. T., J. M. Ivancevich, and S. V. Smith. 1984. Relation of Type A behavior to performance and satisfaction among sales personnel. *Journal of Vocational Behavior* 25:203–14.

McClelland, D. C. 1961. *The Achieving Society*. New York: Free Press.

———. 1987. *Human Motivation*. Cambridge, Eng.: Cambridge University Press.

McClelland, D. C., J. W. Atkinson, R. A. Clark, and E. L. Lowell. 1976. *The Achievement Motive*. New York: Irvington.

Pulakos, E. D., and N. Schmitt. 1995. Experience-based and situational interview questions: Studies of validity. *Personnel Psychology* 48:289–308.

Sager, J. K. 1991. Type A behavior pattern (TABP) among salespeople and its relationship to job stress. *Journal of Personal Selling and Sales Management* 11:1–14.

Schulman, P. 1995. Explanatory style and achievement in school and work. In *Explanatory Style,* ed. G. M. Buchanan and M. Seligman, 253–80. New Jersey: Erlbaum.

———. 1999. Applying learned optimism to increase sales productivity. *Journal of Personal Selling and Sales Management* 19:31–37.

Seligman, M. E. P., and P. Schulman. 1986. Explanatory style as a predictor of productivity and quitting among life insurance sales agents. *Journal of Personality and Social Psychology* 50:832–38.

Soyer, R. B., J. L. Rovenpor, and R. E. Kopelman. 1999. Narcissism and achievement motivation as related to three facets of the sales role: attraction, satisfaction, and performance. *Journal of Business and Psychology* 14:285–304.

Spence, J. T., and R. L. Helmreich. 1983. Achievement- related motives and behavior. In *Achievement and Achievement Motives: Psychological and Sociological Approaches,* ed. J. T. Spence, 7–74. San Francisco: Freeman.

Strutton, D., and J. R. Lumpkin. 1993. The relationship between optimism and coping styles of salespeople. *Journal of Personal Selling and Sales Management* 13:71–82.

Tucker-Ladd, C. 1997. *Psychological Self-Help.* Mental Help Net. http://mentalhelp.net/psyhelp/ (accessed April 4, 2006).

Van Iddekinge, C. H., P. H. Raymark, and P. L. Roth. 2005. Assessing personality with a structured employment interview: Construct-related validity and susceptibility to response inflation. *Journal of Personality and Social Psychology* 90:536–52.

Vinchur, A. J., J. S. Schippman, F. S. Switzer, and P. L. Roth. 1998. A meta-analytic review of predictors of job performance for salespeople. *Journal of Applied Psychology* 83:586–97.

Witmer, N. T., and J. C. Grip. 2002. *Red Flags in Hiring and Promotion.* Witmer & Associates. www.witmerassociates.com/content.php?ID=29 (accessed August 1, 2005).

Index

SalesDrive, LLC specializes in the testing and interviewing of candidates for sales positions. Its proprietary processes are designed to identify Drive, as well as other fundamental characteristics common to high-performing salespeople.

For more information, please visit
 www.salesdrive.info
or contact Dr. Christopher Croner
at (630) 288-3580.